1

About The Author

Scott Warren spent over 29 years as an entertainment industry executive leading in arenas and performing arts centers in the United States and Canada, and has now transitioned into the pharmaceutical industry. Scott's Christian faith has been, and remains, at the center of his professional and personal life. As an elder at his home church in Orlando, Florida, he serves and leads in a variety of capacities. Scott is married to Whitney and has three daughters and one son.

1 Timothy 1:12 (NLT)

"I thank Christ Jesus our Lord, who has given me strength to do his work. He considered me trustworthy and appointed me to serve him"

PREACH WHERE YOU REACH

Bring Your Jesus to Work (*Every*) Day

SCOTT WARREN

CONTENTS

PREFACE

I was 20,000 feet in the air, on my way to Los Angeles...

As I was listening to a worship music playlist and reading a book by T.D. Jakes, I heard God speak to me. "Write the book", He said. I don't know about you, but when God speaks to me, it freaks me out a little. It was so clear and yet, I needed a little more information.
"Write *what* book?", I respectfully whispered back in my head. God showed me an image of me speaking in my Bible College class that my wife and I had attended every Monday night for two years. I'd recently spoken on Christian leadership and how I incorporate my faith in my own workplace; how my faith guides my decisions and influences the culture I've created. God said "yep, that's the book". I may be paraphrasing.

Out of pure obedience, "**Preach Where You Reach**" was born. Throughout the course of my workweek, I interacted with politicians, clients, agents, contractors and more. This book is a glimpse into my professional life and how I incorporate my faith in all aspects.

I truly believe that when you are obedient to what God is asking you to do, the results will land where they need to land. Throughout the writing of "**Preach Where You Reach**", I had a number of unintended conversations with Christian business leaders that struggled with how to incorporate their faith in their respective workplace. In those conversations, God revealed to me why He wanted me to write this book.

This book is for all you marketplace apostles who want to bring your Jesus to work every day, and a testimony to what obedience to God looks like for me.

INTRODUCTION

Have you ever had a moment, or moments, in your workplace where you thought "this place needs Jesus!"? Or, "this *person* needs Jesus!"? If I'm being completely honest, I'm sure I was on the receiving end of that statement on one more than one occasion.

I read somewhere that 30% of our lives will be spent working. That's 1/3 of our lives! And throughout our careers we will encounter co-workers, direct reports or bosses that become instrumental in our growth and development and, in some cases, life-long friends. But we will also encounter co-workers, direct reports or bosses that test our patience and our "religion".

Regardless of occupation, regardless of whether we have "blue collar" or "white collar" jobs, we will encounter similar experiences in the workplace. Our place of work can be filled with employees celebrating promotions, weddings, the birth of a child, a new client. But our place of work can also be filled with jealousy, gossip, backstabbing, negativity, affairs and greed. Our sin nature is on full display for all to see. All of us have likely experienced a situation in our workplace where we believed the Word of God or the presence of God could change the workplace, or a co-worker, for the better.

As a disciple and follower of Christ, it is our mandate to strive to be more like Jesus in every aspect of our lives. And yet when we go to work each day, it's almost as if we've left that intrinsic part of who we are at the door. We do this for a number of reasons, but I find it really comes down to two main obstacles. Firstly, we don't know how to bring Jesus into the workplace without getting all Jesus-y (yes I know it's not a word, but work with me here) and secondly, and perhaps most importantly, we don't want to get fired!

A general rule that we often hear is, never talk about politics or religion, and certainly not in the workplace. But I'm here to tell you, there are ways that your deep, abiding faith can come to work with you and not only guide your decisions, but influence the entire organization. But don't stop there! Perhaps you interact with customers, suppliers, media, Boards or investors. What is your sphere of influence? Who do you encounter on a daily basis? You can *Preach Where You Reach*!

There are two key points to understand as you read this book. Firstly, what do I mean by "preach"? I think most people, when they hear the word preach, think of delivering a sermon. But the Merriam-Webster Dictionary also defines "preach" as "to advocate earnestly". This is the context which I use. I'm not suggesting you preach the Good News in the workplace, but I am encouraging you to advocate, or publicly recommend and display, the characteristics or qualities of Christ in a sincere, authentic way in the workplace. In other words, preach the gospel with your life. Secondly, it would be easy to take the Christ-like characteristics recommended in this book out of context. It would be easy to believe that if anyone just demonstrates these characteristics in your sphere of influence, you are establishing a Christ-centered workplace. It simply isn't true. This books presumes you are a faith-filled, Holy Spirit-filled believer. The characteristics I discuss in this book, taken on their own, would amount to just works. As a believer, we understand that we need faith *and* works. In James 2:19-20 NLT, it says *"You say you have faith, for you believe there is one God. Good for you! Even the demons believe this, and they tremble in terror. How foolish! Can't you see that faith without good deeds is useless?"* The opposite is also true. Good deeds, or works, are useless without faith.

We are made in the image of God. And as such, the Christ-like attributes that we'll uncover in this book aren't only in Christ; they are in you and me! I wrote this book to encourage you. Each of us can be leaders in our workplace, with Christ-centered principles. I've seen "Bring Your Kids to Work Day" and "Bring Your Dog to Work Day." As Christians, we should certainly bring our Jesus to work every day. Now let's take a look at how I've done that, and how you can too.

one

Seeds

Luke 8:15 (ESV)

"As for that in the good soil, they are those who, hearing the word, hold it fast in an honest and good heart, and bear fruit with patience".

Seeds

I never cared much for church. Well, I never really went to church growing up, except for special occasions, like weddings or funerals. As I got older, I would go sporadically, mostly out of curiosity. I remember when I lived in Ocean City, Maryland, I decided to give St. Paul's By The Sea a try. Mainly because I could wear shorts and flip flops. Sand in the toes and God seemed like a winning combination. When I would go, either out of obligation or curiosity, and regardless of church location, I always walked away with the same feeling. Well, actually, it was a lack of feeling anything at all. And I didn't get a sense that anyone else was feeling anything either. It seemed cold and robotic. When the priest said X, the people responded with Y. Everyone knew the routine. They stood up at the same time. They sat down at the same time. I went enough to know the Lord's Prayer and was able to recite it in unison with everyone else. And when the priest said "Peace be with you", I could respond with "and also with you." I went to a Catholic service not long ago, and they changed the response on me! The response now is "and also with your spirit". Just when I thought I knew what I was doing, curve ball!

The church, as a building, always fascinated me. The majesty of the architecture was awe-inspiring. The beauty of the stained-glass windows would captivate me and I would get lost in the images, though I didn't really know what they represented, with the exception of the crucifixion. I remember seeing confessionals, and just the sight of them brought an overwhelming sense of guilt and shame. I never went into one of those to spill my guts or confess my sins. I always figured God knew what I was up to anyway. No matter which church I attended, I saw robes and candles and heard pipe organs and hymns. The church seemed so full of pageantry, and yet I left feeling empty. I always believed in God and Jesus, but I had never actually encountered them in any church I'd attended.

I did read the Bible, or parts of it, on occasion. And I believe it was Leviticus that finally pulled me away from the church and began my crusade to debate any Christian I would encounter. I was one of those people who knew enough of the Bible to be dangerous. Perhaps "ignorant" would be a better label. Because I didn't understand what I was reading, I placed it in my own context and lashed out at believers for their hypocrisy. "Leviticus says shellfish are an abomination and yet your church is having a crab feast. Hypocrite!", I'd say. Man, was I proud in my ignorance.

Seeds

I was far from understanding old covenant/new covenant. I just saw preachers "fall from grace" by stealing from the church, having affairs or molesting children. I wanted no part of it.

My distaste for the church was well understood in my family. It certainly made for lively discussions around the holidays. I remember one Thanksgiving in particular. My Aunt, who did her best to have grace and patience for my unwavering arrogance, declared prayer works. "Scott, I have a friend who was sick and we created a prayer circle and prayed for healing and guess what? She's better", she said with authority. I responded, in true Scott fashion. "I'm guessing you prayed for my grandmother too and guess what? She's dead now". It's ok if you want to face palm right now. I'll even give you a minute to reflect on whether this was the right book for you. I do promise that if you stick with me here, it gets better. Even I'm shaking my head right now!

Fast forward to my move to Hamilton, Ontario. I was the same ol' Scott, but I was about to encounter Jenn. Not only does God have a sense of humor, but he has a plan. Let me explain. Jenn became my Executive Assistant. Jenn was also a worship leader at a local church. This was about to get entertaining!

Preach Where You Reach: Bring Your Jesus to Work (*Every*) Day

I don't know how it began, but I remember Jenn and I having conversations about church. It wasn't long before she discovered her boss had a Goliath-sized ignorance and attitude regarding church. But she knew how that story ended. Instead of throwing a stone at my head she opted for a more subtle approach. Over the next few months she was a farmer, planting seeds. At the time, I was living in a hotel, until my family would arrive from Cleveland. Jenn invited me over to have dinner with her and her husband and children. When I arrived, she let me know that she had invited some friends to come over as well. I was in a new city and didn't know anyone, so I welcomed the opportunity to meet more people. I ended up having an amazing evening of great food and lots of laughter and I looked forward to seeing them all again soon. What I didn't know at the time, was all of these friends she introduced me to went to her church as well. She's so stealth!

As the Canadian winter turned to spring and then into summer, Jenn invited me to her church's annual picnic. I just imagined everyone sitting around on picnic tables reading the Bible. I wanted no part of that and politely declined. Jenn received my response with warmth and kindness. Another seed planted.

Seeds

My family arrived from Cleveland and we began our new lives in Canada. Due to restrictions with my work visa and my family's resident visas, my wife was not permitted to work in Canada. While that may sound amazing for her, she had worked all her life and really enjoyed her career. Initially, she got to spend the summer with the kids at home, but it wasn't long before school started.

I would go to work, my wife, Whitney, would walk the kids to school and then she was home alone. Whitney knew no one. She was in a new country with no friends, no job and she was miserable. The kids had a difficult time adjusting as well and I was putting in long hours as I began to build the culture of my new workplace. But I was hurting. I removed my family from the comfort of their home and school and friends and dropped them in a new country and spent most of my time working. The guilt and regret I felt ate at me day after day.

A few months later, Christmas was approaching. Jenn let me know that her church was having a Christmas production and she would be singing. She invited me and encouraged me to bring my family. While I had little interest in the church service itself, I wanted to hear Jenn sing. I wanted to encourage her and I knew it would mean a lot to her if I came to the service. I remember it vividly. The snow was coming down and the thought of staying inside in the warmth and watching a movie was pretty tempting. Whitney was nervous about driving in the snow and said she didn't want to go to the church, not in these conditions. I pleaded with Whitney saying "I've said no to Jenn so many times when asked to go to church. I really want to be there to show my support. I want to go." Whitney agreed and we loaded up the kids and drove to the church.

I had never seen a church quite like this one. There wasn't a single stained-glass window in sight. In fact, the church was in an old coal gas plant that was easily over 150 years old. The building, once derelict and left in ruin, was restored to its former glory by the church. We walked into the building and were greeted by people that seemed to be expecting us. They were kind, but kind in a true, authentic way. This didn't seem like church as I knew it. There were no pews, candles or pipe organ. There was a stage and room for about 75 guests. It was intimate and the kindness of the people gave the night a warmth that contradicted the snowfall outside.

The lights dimmed and the worship band began. Guitars, drums, bass, keyboards and Jenn, my Executive

Seeds

Assistant, at center stage. The sound and lights rivaled any small club show I had seen. Lyrics were projected on screens and the congregation sang along with a passion and emotion I had never seen before. Arms raised in the air across the room. And Jenn was amazing! I felt an overwhelming emotion as tears rolled down my cheeks. My wife leaned over to me and said "why are you crying?." *"I don't know!"*, I responded, puzzled.

As worship ended, I realized it was the first time I had felt something in church. It was unfamiliar. *And the service had just begun!* The Senior Pastor took the stage to deliver the message for the evening. He was in his late forties, but seemed younger. His clothes were trendy without being absurd. He delivered the message with humor and emotion. The message was relatable and practical. It was refreshing. "This is what church can be like?", I thought. As the service was coming to an end, the pastor instructed every head bowed and every eye closed. He said "if you would like to know this Jesus we've talked about tonight; if you'd like to have a relationship with this Jesus, on the count of three, I'd like you to just raise your hand and put it back down. One. Two. Three. As he reached Three, my wife and I looked down the row at our children. I couldn't believe my eyes. My six-year-old son,

Dublin, had his hand in the air. Tears fell from my eyes. In that moment, there was a paradigm shift. We had provided so much for our children, but clearly there was a need, or desire, we weren't meeting. Our children wanted a relationship with Jesus.

We came to the Christmas service to encourage my Executive Assistant. We left having encountered the overwhelming presence of God.

Even though I had never encountered God in a traditional church building, I certainly didn't expect to find him in an old coal/gas plant. I've come to understand that God will meet you right where you are. You can be in a converted Chinese restaurant and God will pour out His presence like sake.

A farmer in the midwest might plant his corn in May, but the harvest doesn't come until October. An apple tree can take anywhere from 3-8 years to bear fruit. But you can be certain that nothing grows unless a seed is planted. Jenn continued to plant seeds within me with each seemingly dead-end conversation; with a dinner at her home; with each decline of an invitation to church or a picnic. She was subtle. She was kind. She was patient.

Seeds

And in God's timing, she witnessed the harvest. My wife and I, and our children, all gave our lives to Christ.

Regardless of my positions throughout my various career stops over the past 29 years, my leadership style has remand relatively unchanged. The difference now, having come to Christ, is I now know why I lead the way I do and for whom I lead.

It's easy to have an impact on your workplace. You can have a positive impact. You can have a negative impact. You also have the opportunity to make a Kingdom impact. Like Jenn, when you Preach Where You Reach, you can impact not only the lives of those you work alongside, but you can change the trajectory of generations to come.

In your organization, you can have a dramatic affect on the culture. You don't need to be the CEO. You can begin by leading your respective area and building a culture within your department. And while you have the freedom to set your own culture, that freedom comes with responsibility. As much as you can establish a positive, life-giving culture, you can also establish a culture based on our sin nature.

The culture you create is like soil. We can look to Matthew 13:1-9 (NLT) for insight:

13 Later that same day Jesus left the house and sat beside the lake. 2 A large crowd soon gathered around him, so he got into a boat. Then he sat there and taught as the people stood on the shore. 3 He told many stories in the form of parables, such as this one: "Listen! A farmer went out to plant some seeds. 4 As he scattered them across his field, some seeds fell on a footpath, and the birds came and ate them. 5 Other seeds fell on shallow soil with underlying rock. The seeds sprouted quickly because the soil was shallow. 6 But the plants soon wilted under the hot sun, and since they didn't have deep roots, they died. 7 Other seeds fell among thorns that grew up and choked out the tender plants. 8 Still other seeds fell on fertile soil, and they produced a crop that was thirty, sixty, and even a hundred times as much as had been planted! 9 Anyone with ears to hear should listen and understand."

In order for us to flourish as God has called us, the soil of our own hearts must be fertile so that we can receive the Word of God and and establish a deep root system. The same is true for the culture you create in your workplace. When you create a culture of aerated, fertile soil, the seeds you plant will produce an abundant harvest.

Whether you've recently been promoted, have come into a new work environment or you just want to bring your faith to the workplace, the first thing I would encourage you to do is establish a Christ-centered culture. That doesn't mean that you mandate prayer and make employees only listen to worship music. It means to take Christ-like qualities and they become your foundation. Many of these qualities I'll cover in this book may seem passive or more touchy-feely. But understand that Jesus was a lion and a lamb. There are times when you have to be direct and matter-of-fact. There will be times when you will need to discipline an employee. Your workplace is a business that needs to see results and meet goals, financial and otherwise. But in those moments of correction, you are approaching those situations through the lens of Jesus.

Establishing a Christ-centered culture is not meant to only stay within the walls of your workplace. I approach everyone I reach with the same foundation. Whether I am talking with the Mayor, a health inspector, a TV anchor, a corporate partner or a potential client, I am employing the same Christ-centered culture in that relationship.

And the culture doesn't begin and end with me. Every one of my Directors used the same Christ-like principles whether they label it as such or not. Whether they recognize them as Christ-like attributes or not, they were treating their relationships with kindness, compassion, humility and gratitude.

You don't have to publicly declare that you lead a Christ-centered workplace or that you bring Jesus to work. You just have to let the light of Jesus shine through as you go through your workday. There will be plenty of opportunity to profess your faith. I have yet to encounter a workplace where someone doesn't ask how your weekend was or what you did over the weekend. It's a great opportunity to say "we went to church on Sunday and then went for a hike with friends" or whatever you do after church. But I never miss an opportunity to say I went to church, or served at church, when I'm asked about my weekend.

Seeds

Opportunities to mention your faith will come. It's what you do with the opportunity that matters. A couple of years ago, we had a number of events that were scheduled suddenly cancel or move to the following year. It happens. There isn't anything I could do about it, but it was going to hurt our bottom line considerably. An employee came to me and said "How is it that you stay so calm when everything seems to be falling apart?" I said, "Because of my faith, I am believing that those cancelled events are clearing the way for something better to come along. And that brings me peace." I didn't have to get into a deeper conversation about Jesus. I was just able to subtly plant a seed. I declared my faith and, for a moment, she received my Christ-centered perspective.

It all starts with establishing a Christ-centered culture. Build your business or your department on the solid foundation of Jesus Christ. When you do, you will see the fruit. This fruit will be visible in energetic, passionate, dedicated employees. The fruit will be visible in better relationships with clients, corporate partners and suppliers. As a believer, you know that this foundation doesn't prevent difficulties in your business, but it will be an anchor when the waves of adversity come crashing.

Preach Where You Reach: Bring Your Jesus to Work (*Every*) Day

And you will be surrounded by a workforce that chooses to be in the boat with you when the storms arise.

two

Sticky Shoes

1 Peter 5:3-4 (NLT)

3*"Don't lord it over the people assigned to your care, but lead them by your own good example. ***4***And when the Great Shepherd appears, you will receive a crown of never-ending glory and honor"*

Sticky Shoes

I moved to Hamilton, Ontario from Cleveland, Ohio when the company I worked for took over management of a city-owned arena and theatre. It was the end of February. I know, seems like a poor time of year to move to Canada. But coming from Cleveland, it wasn't too dissimilar. My wife, Whitney, and our kids were still back in the States while the kids finished school and I figured out this new city and country in which we would be living. Celsius, kilometres and bags of milk (that's right, I said *bags* of milk!) were all new experiences for me. I vividly recall one night in particular, as I watched the evening news. The weather man said there was a snow storm. He said something like "There's a snowstorm about 50 kilometres away and it's heading for us. And with temps at -5C, we'll likely see 20 centimetres of snow." *What?!! What are you saying to me?!! How far away is this storm? How cold is it? How many inches are we expecting?!*

I was the General Manager. I had been assigned Directors that I had never met, with the exception of one, as well as additional full-time staff and a large contingent of part-time staff. No one, at this point, knew me at all and they certainly didn't know my leadership style. It would be honest to say, many of my part-time staff likely didn't even know my name.

I met with as many of the part-time staff as possible, during a "town hall" style gathering to introduce myself and my Directors. I let them know that while there was a hierarchy and an organizational chart, I viewed the chart to be more of a flat line. Each of us brought a unique skill-set that contributes to the bigger picture and success of the organization. I could read the look of mistrust on their faces. After introductions of my leadership team and painting a vision of where we would be taking the organization, the wheels came off. The meeting began to turn into complaints that had clearly been bubbling under the surface for quite some time. It was clear that they heard what I said, but I got the sense that seeing was believing.

A couple of weeks passed and we began a weeklong run of Disney on Ice in the arena. On Saturday, we had three shows with a short turnaround between shows. That short turnaround meant we needed "all hands on deck" to pick up all the empty popcorn containers, drink cups, nacho trays and hot dog wrappers the guests had left behind. I went to the custodian's staging area, put on plastic gloves and grabbed a couple of large trash bags.

Sticky Shoes

Then, in my suit and tie, my Directors and I began to go row by row putting litter in the large trash bags. At one point I looked up. Looking back at me were stares of disbelief from our part-time staff. I put my head back down and kept going.

After dragging leaking trash bags to the large receptacle and removing my plastic gloves I walked back to the concourse. The snow-cone juice residue made it so that, while my feet wanted to walk, the bottom of my shoes weren't making it easy. Just then, an older female usher came up to me and said, "Excuse me. I've worked here for 19 years and I have never seen anyone from management help clean up. I just wanted to say thank you." Another said "I've been here nine years and I've never seen people in your position help us." Yet another said, "I guess you were serious when you said we are all equal." The work needed to be done and I was more than capable of helping, like everyone else. I could have used my position and watched as my staff did the dirty work. But instead, I wanted to show them what serving and working together really meant and so I got to work. I didn't do this to send a message, but it certainly did. The Greek word for humble is tapeinóō. It literally means to make, or become, low. I find that there is something freeing about laying down I find that there is something freeing about laying down your position, or authority, and becoming like those you lead. The irony, of course, is that by "becoming low", you are viewed higher in the eyes, and hearts, of those you lead.

The undisputed champion of humility was, of course, Jesus. The Son of God, God in the flesh came to us as a baby in a manger. Just typing that felt romantic. A manger. Of course, we can picture this manger in our heads because we've seen it so many times on Christmas cards, nativity displays or in adorable elementary school plays. Joseph and Mary, the wise men and maybe a sheep or two and throw in a camel for good measure, surround baby Jesus. Jesus is lying peacefully on a bed of hay, swaddled in a blanket. Sounds amazing right? Well, except for the bed of hay. That *had* to be itchy!

Some biblical scholars describe the birthplace of Jesus as abhorrent conditions with animal filth, feces and the like. Other biblical scholars believe that Christ was born in a peasant home on the first floor, where animals were kept at night. In either case, the conditions were certainly not what we would expect to be the birthplace of the Messiah. I know for my own children, I made sure my

Sticky Shoes

wife and I had a private room at the hospital with a TV and cable. I made sure we had a pullout bed or a chair that converted to a bed. I mean, even though my wife did all the work, *I wanted to be comfortable too*!

But we're not talking about my children; we're talking about our Lord and Saviour. I can picture baby Jesus being born in a palatial palace with marble columns, gold fixtures with bronze statues dotting the palace grounds and groves of fruit trees; Mary being assisted by the most skilled physicians in the land and Jesus being swaddled in the finest silk garments and placed gently into the most beautifully adorned bassinet. And this would only begin to touch on the type of extravagance that would be fitting for the birth of Jesus. But as God always does, He used this moment to teach us a lesson about what's truly important. So, instead of coming into the world as obvious royalty, as we would know it, He positioned Him low, in a feed box!

Throughout Christ's ministry, examples of His humility abound. One of the greatest examples that we read in the Bible comes at the end of Christ's ministry. Jerusalem is crowded with those celebrating Passover. Word gets out that Jesus is on His way to Jerusalem and the crowds lined the streets, ready to receive the Messiah. Jesus instructs two of his disciples to get a donkey from a nearby village and meet him. Jesus mounted the donkey and rode it into Jerusalem as pilgrims waved palm branches, as a sign of victory, and laid down their coats in the street in awe of their King. The donkey, in that time, was a symbol of peace. Jesus didn't ride in on a warhorse or a horse befitting a king. He came to Jerusalem, humbly and in peace, preparing for his mission and purpose to be complete.

In Philippians 2:5-11 (NLT) we read:

5 "You must have the same attitude that Christ Jesus had. 6 Though he was God, he did not think of equality with God as something to cling to. 7 Instead, he gave up his divine privileges; he took the humble position of a slave and was born as a human being. When he appeared in human form, 8 he humbled himself in obedience to God and died a criminal's death on a cross. 9 Therefore, God elevated him to the place of highest honor and gave him the name above all other names, 10 that at the name of Jesus every knee should bow, in heaven and on earth and under the earth, 11 and every tongue declare that Jesus Christ is Lord, to the glory of God the Father".

Sticky Shoes

Wow! That's a mic drop moment, when we speak of being humble. I mean, what can I really say to follow that? I guess the only option I really have is to use some ridiculous real life example that shows how this plays out in my life. Baseball!

My son, Dublin, loves baseball. And he's a really gifted little athlete. He's fun to watch. Dublin plays shortstop for our region's premier baseball travel team. When it's game time, he's zoned in. Before the ball is pitched he knows exactly what he's doing with the ball if it comes his way. He's seemingly played every possible scenario out in his head. And when the ball comes his way, he stops at nothing to make the play. One year, Dublin won Defensive Player of the Year. And it was no contest. But, if I say, "Hey Dublin – Luke?" he says "14:11." It's been drilled into him by my wife and me. Luke 14:11 says "For those who exalt themselves will be humbled, and those who humble themselves will be exalted." This past season we saw this play out in actions, not just words.

During a tournament game, Dublin was on fire. He had a great bat, his glove was like a vacuum, stopping every ball that came his way. Diving catches, barehanded grabs and more. During this tournament, the opposing team's coaches determine a Play of the Game winner and honor the child with a medal to signify the accomplishment. In a game the day before, Dublin was honored with this medal. But here we were again and his game was unbelievable. The opposing team's coaches gathered and after giving accolades and praise to this young ballplayer, they awarded the Play of the Game medal to Dublin. Dublin went up to the coaches and received the medal. But what happened next made my heart full and my tears fall. Dublin immediately turned around and walked to another teammate and gave him the medal. Dublin said "I already have one and you made a great play in left field." I have to say, it's moments like this that make you feel like you must be doing something right.

So, in addition to the sticky shoes story earlier, how have I put this Christ-like attribute into action in my workplace? Like most things that seem complicated, the answers are rather simple.

In our Boardroom, we had an enormous round table. I mean, enormous! You would have to break this table into smaller pieces to remove it from the room. One small section of this round table was made solid to the ground. In other words, no one can sit in this one small section because you couldn't put your legs under the table. I'm told the design is modeled in a way that whoever is at the

Sticky Shoes

"head" of this round table would have no one that could oppose him/her on the other side. So, for many leaders, there would be an obvious place for the CEO or GM, in my case, to sit. Whenever I had a meeting in this room, I always sat *anywhere* but at the implied "head" of the table. I didn't want my seat location to determine my leadership position; I wanted my vision and actions to make that clear.

One September, we were having a huge season kick-off party with full-time and part-time staff. Our season typically ran from September through May, with a sprinkling of events throughout the summer months. This gathering would be an opportunity for me to address all the employees and layout my expectations for the season. Expectations like helping carry food or drinks for a guest whose hands could barely hold the popcorn, nachos and drinks. Seeing a guest who is about to take a picture of their family and asking them if we can take the picture so all of the family can be in the photo. As I walked into the arena to see the set-up, I noticed a small stage and a podium from which I was supposed to give my remarks. I told my staff, "I won't be speaking from up there". I wanted to be on the ground and walking around the tables where the staff would be sitting. I wanted to be seen as someone they *wanted* to work for, not someone they *do* work for. I find, when you take away the perception of pretense, you become relatable. When you exemplify servant leadership, your staff will go out of their way for you. Of course, it still needs to be clear that you are in a position of authority. But, as I said earlier, when you become low, you are viewed higher in the eyes of those you lead.

I also have the clichéd "open door policy". Any employee of mine, regardless of position within the organization, knows that they can come to me at any time if they have something important to them that they want me to hear or get my opinion/direction. Unless I'm on the phone or my office door is closed, I make myself available.

I once had an issue that I was struggling with and I called the President of the company for which I worked. I left him a voicemail just saying that I had an issue I wanted to discuss and I asked him to call me when he had a moment. Within 15 minutes, my phone rang and it was him. I said, "I'm really sorry about this. I know you have more pressing issues to deal with than my situation" and he stopped me and said, "Scott, right now, you are the most important thing I've got. How can I help?" I'll never forget that, because he was accessible.

If you have a pressing project or deadline, close your door. Otherwise, be open and ready to make your employee feel like the most important person in that moment. Who knows, it may open up an opportunity to speak life into their situation.

Matthew 25:37-40 (NLT)

37*"Then these righteous ones will reply, 'Lord, when did we ever see you hungry and feed you? Or thirsty and give you something to drink?* **38***Or a stranger and show you hospitality? Or naked and give you clothing?* **39***When did we ever see you sick or in prison and visit you?'* **40***"And the King will say, 'I tell you the truth, when you did it to one of the least of these my brothers and sisters, you were doing it to me!'*

About a year after the sticky shoes episode, Disney on Ice was back again (what is it with this show?!). As I approached the arena, there was a man, who appeared to be homeless, sitting on the ground and leaning up against the venue. I had observed him over the past several months as he courteously extended pleasantries to passers-by. "Enjoy the show!" he'd say. "Be careful driving home". He had a hat placed on the ground in front of him, but he never asked for money.

The sun was shining, but it was still March in Canada so the air still had a bit of a sting to it. I walked up to the man, dressed in my suit and tie, and as his eyes met mine, I sat down next to him. I extended my hand and said "Hi, I'm Scott. I run the arena here." He immediately got nervous and tripped over his words as he said "I don't bother anyone, I promise! The police know me. They know I don't bother anybody." I said "It's ok, it's ok. I know you don't. I'm actually a big fan of yours. What's your name?" "Neil", he said, still nervous. His beard was unruly and his clothes tattered. "I notice that you never ask for money and you are always so kind to everyone that walks by and I wanted to thank you", I said. "Can I ask you a question? And you don't have to answer if you don't want to. But, what happened? What happened in your life that brought you to this point?"

With a slight hesitation, he said "Well, I was raised by very religious parents and they would often beat me. I got beat a lot. And to cope with that, I turned to crack. It got out of control and now I'm here. I still slip up every now and then. Um, I don't really want to talk about it any-more." As I stood up I said "Neil, it's really nice to meet you" and I walked inside.

Sticky Shoes

It would have been easy to walk passed Neil. I could have demanded he get off of my property. I could have asked him to stop bothering our guests. But the Holy Spirit led me to sit down next to him and get to know him. Fast forward three years and picture Neil as a guest in my suite for a concert with Canadian legends, The Tragically Hip. Drumming on the granite countertop and rocking out to every song. He had an amazing time. Same Neil. Same me. Same God.

When you truly surrender your life to Christ; when you say "God, I've tried to do it my way for so long, I'm done. I turn my life back over to you. Holy Spirit, guide my steps, guide my words, guide my actions. Help me get closer to you, God. Help me live a Christ-centered life and bring Your Word to life in my everyday interactions", your prayer will be answered. But you'll have to be obedient to it.

The Holy Spirit told me to take a moment and spend some time with this disheveled man that sits on the ground outside of my arena. Get to know him. Give him an opportunity to be heard. Give him an opportunity to be somebody, not just a nameless "vagrant". And I obeyed. That was the pivotal moment. In that interaction on the cold pavement, a bond was created. Neil now knows my wife and children. He still sits outside the arena on event days. But now, he's not "that man", he's Neil. And I believe, wholeheartedly, that God has a reason for us being in each other's lives. And I'm grateful.

Remember, bringing Jesus to work and leading a Christ-centered workplace is not limited to your employees. Neil didn't work for me, but I encountered him *because* of my work. He was in my workplace "footprint", or my circle of influence. Preach Where You Reach is about letting Christ work through you in every aspect of your workplace and any extension of that workplace.

When you lead with humility, you are bringing Jesus to work

three

Pain Has a Purpose

Colossians 3:12-13 (NLT)

12"Since God chose you to be the holy people he loves, you must clothe yourselves with tenderhearted mercy, kindness, humility, gentleness, and patience. 13 Make allowance for each other's faults, and forgive anyone who offends you. Remember, the Lord forgave you, so you must forgive others"

Pain Has a Purpose

I love the Bible. You can read one verse and dissect each God-breathed word. You can get lost in it. You can be found in it. You can use it as a mirror reflecting your own life and measure how well you're doing. You can let it marinate and just soak up its essence. You can extract wisdom. You can live it.

In the verse on the previous page, it would be easy to just read it quickly and move on to the next. But let's look at this for a moment. "Since God chose you", ok stop! See, we didn't get very far. *God chose you*! For most of us, that in and of itself is a revelation. The verse then goes on to say "to be the holy people he loves". God *loves* us! We can be so busy hating ourselves that we completely miss these life-giving words. We're so busy living and dwelling on our past failures and disappointments that it's hard for us to believe we are loved by anyone, let alone by God.

But I love the next part of this verse. Scripture says "you must clothe yourselves with tenderhearted mercy, kindness, humility, gentleness, and patience". We could just read that quickly and say, "I get it, I need to be nice". But the word I want to focus on for a minute is *clothe*. Paul, who wrote the book of Colossians, isn't just saying we should do these things. He's saying we should clothe ourselves with them. When we put on a shirt or pants (or a cashmere sweater, because they are *so soft*!), we cover ourselves. We put ourselves entirely within. So when we look at these instructions for life, we are told to completely envelop ourselves in these qualities. These characteristics aren't something for us to do; they are something for us to be.

When Paul wrote this letter to the people of Colosse, a city about 120 miles from Ephasus, he was in a Roman prison for preaching the Good News. Because of the city's location, on one of the main Roman roads of the region, the Colossians would have likely been exposed to various religious and philosophical teachings and beliefs. As a result, the people of Colosse were straying from having Christ at the center of their lives. Paul was writing to the Colossians to try to refocus their hearts and minds on the ways of Christ.

Paul certainly encourages the Colossians in this letter, but he also gives very clear directions. Paul says "you must clothe yourselves with tenderhearted mercy, kindness, humility, gentleness, and patience." He isn't saying you *should* do this. He says you *must*. As Christian business leaders, we have the same mandate. As we look to bring Jesus to work, we must clothe ourselves in these qualities.

All of these qualities, in this context, could be summarized as compassion. Compassion is love displayed when we encounter those that are experiencing suffering, pain, sadness, heartache or grief. You will undoubtedly come across this in your workplace. We all experience these emotions and they don't go away when we step through the office door.

Being a strong leader requires managing employee's abilities, passions and motivations to best position them, and the company, to meet specific objectives. But because we are human, being a strong leader also requires us to be aware and attentive to our employee's emotional states as well. I've gotta tell you, this Christ-like characteristic is likely the one I have built my career on the most.

I'm a crier. I often like to blame it on the dust in the air or a yawn, but I don't think anyone has ever believed those excuses. I'd like to think perhaps it was Oprah's fault. When she gave cars to everyone, I was destroyed! I've never been the same. I joke, sort of. I've always been a little (or a lot) more emotional than others. Truth be told, I've always really disliked this part of myself. I used to say "I need to tighten this stuff up".

Ok, I didn't always say 'stuff', but you get the point. I always saw it as a negative. When I would present someone with an Employee of the Month acknowledgment, I'd get emotional. I'd even tell myself before I gave the speech, "C'mon Scott. You've got this. You can do it!" Perhaps personal pep talks aren't my specialty, because it never worked. As soon as I started in on my heartfelt message, I would begin to get emotional. Now let's be clear, I don't become a sobbing mess in a ball on the floor. That would just be weird! But I will get teary-eyed and need to pause and try to regain my composure.

As I said, this has driven me crazy almost my entire career. "Leaders don't get emotional", I'd tell myself. "Leaders certainly don't cry", I'd whisper in my head. All of that changed as a result of three distinct moments.

The first moment that was a revelation in my "emotional man recovery" (EMR. Likely not an official medical or psychological condition but let's go with it) came during a book study with the men of my church. We were reading

Pain Has a Purpose

"Loose That Man and Let Him Go!" by T.D. Jakes. I don't know about you, but I can read a book like that and there could be one paragraph or one sentence that just shakes you to the core. This book was so full of wisdom and yet it was seven simple words that changed my thinking. These seven words are articulated in the Bible as well. *Jesus was a lion and a lamb.* That's it. Really. In that moment, I realized that what I had wanted to change for so long, was actually supposed to be part of my DNA as a brother of Christ. We share the same bloodline. Jesus is the example I should follow, not some earthly thinking of how a man should or shouldn't express emotion. In my pastor's home, surrounded by my brothers in Christ while reading a T.D. Jakes book, I started to change my paradigm. But it was a work in progress.

The second moment of revelation in my EMR, came in a staff meeting. This moment is actually a little fuzzy for me and yet parts of it are crystal clear. I was in our weekly staff meeting with Directors and managers and I read an email of praise I had received regarding a certain employee. I don't remember which employee the email referenced or what the email said. But after the email was read, I went on to praise the employee as well. You can probably guess what happened. I starting tearing up and got emotional. These heartfelt moments just slay me. Afterward I went on with the meeting and when it was over, I went back to my office. About 10 minutes later, there was a knock on my open office door. It was one of our recent hires. He had been with us likely only a month. He said "Can I talk to you for a minute?" I said "sure, come on in." He said "I just wanted to say how much I enjoy working here. I've never seen a leader in the workplace get emotional like you did this morning. I knew this place was different than any other place I've ever worked. And this morning, I saw why. The way people are around here is a clear result of how you lead from the top. I just wanted to say how much seeing that meant to me this morning and I wanted to thank you."

I began to realize that the way my emotions come pouring through my flood gate (like my flood gate is made of Swiss cheese), doesn't only affect me. My heart, my compassion, has the ability to inspire, motivate and deeply impact those that work for me. For so long I attempted to stifle my emotions and here is someone telling me how much my emotions meant to them and how they contributed to his happiness in the workplace. That was revolutionary for me.

Pain Has a Purpose

The third moment was a result of Garth Brooks. Yes, the country singer. Our arena hosted five Garth Brooks shows over four days, including a two show Saturday. So Sunday came and we had the last of the five shows. It was Easter Sunday. I wanted to address our part-time staff, who had worked tirelessly to welcome and serve 80,000 fans over the course of the run. During the pre-event meeting with all of our ushers and ticket-takers, I stood on a chair and began thanking them for all that they did to make these concerts an unprecedented success. Well , here we go again. Scott gets emotional. Shocker! I had to compose myself a few times as I poured out my thanks. As I stepped down from the chair, ushers came up to me one at a time and hugged me and said thank you. "You can tell you really meant it and that means a lot to us", they said. In that brief instant of raw emotion, there was a bond. I could have announced we were going to add a couple more shows and they would have cheered. They felt valued and respected and they knew I meant it.

While there are likely more similar moments that helped me become comfortable with my emotional leadership, these examples stand out to me. The key to leading with compassion is authenticity. I can't manufacture tears. I can't create the crack in my voice or the quivering chin.

These things come from truly caring about the people you lead. Believe me, if you're not authentic, they will know. And you will lose credibility in an instant. Jesus was a lion AND a lamb. I'm finally content with my lamb side (ok, maybe 90% content, I'm still working through it).

As I mentioned earlier, we don't leave our personal lives at home when we come to work. Those that we lead will experience the death of a spouse, child custody battles, illness and so much more. Our workplace was rocked not long ago.

One of our employees, who had previously battled cancer and won, was beginning to have pain in her arm, where cancer once was. In a short period of time, she was in excruciating pain. After going to the doctor for testing, the results came back. The cancer had returned. Not only had the cancer returned, but it looked like her arm would need to be amputated to stop further cancer damage to her body.

Now, there's no business school class you can take to learn how to deal with these moments. There's no business book that can give you the top seven steps to take in these situations. But as a Christian leader, there is one book you can access that can help you, the Bible.

I knew this employee believed in Christ but when we receive news like cancer or amputation, how many know our faith can be tested? So I reached out to her in an email and said:

"Good morning. As the GM, I am greatly affected by the news of anyone on my staff facing adversity, pain or sickness. We are extended family in this workplace. We love and care for each other deeply. The news of your recent results just allows us to love on you greater and let you know that we are there for you, no matter what you need. If I can remove my GM "hat" for a moment, I am also a man of deep abiding faith. It is this faith that allows me the freedom to see that our pain serves a purpose. Your circumstance allows you to tell your testimony – how you battled before and won; how you are able to thrive and flourish regardless of what your body tries to do to hold you back. You have the opportunity to share your story with others that are either going through what you are going through or some similar adversity. You have an opportunity to be the light in a world that lives in so much darkness. I am praying and believing for complete healing and

restoration of body and mind. I am praying and believing for a comfort, strength and peace in the midst of the storms. You are loved and valued here. I am grateful for your life and your story. My family and I will continue to lift you up in prayer."

She replied:

"Thank you Scott for your lovely words, yes I believe things happen for a reason and for whatever reason I am where I should be and have the people around me who for whatever reason are with me to support me and help me through this part of my life. I thank you for your prayers and will do everything in my power to not let this beat me and I too have faith that I will come out of this stronger and more determined than ever. Thank you again it is definitely a help to know I have the love and support of all my colleagues. It means a great deal to me and my family. Many thanks"

Most people, including non-believers, going through something as difficult as this would likely welcome prayer. However, it is very important to know your audience. It's one thing to tell someone you'll keep them in your prayers. It's another entirely to start laying hands on them and speaking in tongues! The relationships you build will help determine how open and raw you can be with your faith in the workplace. Because this employee was a believer, I knew I could speak to her from a position of deep faith. The same was true, post-surgery. I emailed her again a few days after surgery and said:

"Good morning! I just wanted to take a moment in all my busyness to pause and let you know I'm thinking of you and praying for you. You are certainly missed in the office. I understand surgery went well and I am grateful to God for that. If I can be of any assistance, please let me know. Can't wait to get you back into your "extended family" at work. See you soon!"

Shortly after she received this message, she was leaving the hospital after a follow up, and wanted to stop by our staff meeting to see everyone. I can tell you that when she walked into the room, there wasn't a dry eye in the place. Part of that was certainly because we are human, but a big part of that display of emotion was because we had built a culture of compassion. We truly viewed each other as family. When one of us hurt, we all hurt.

As I write this chapter, our work family has experienced another tragedy that has shaken us to our core. The wife of one of our employees was hit by a vehicle as she walked across the street to catch a connecting bus. She sustained a fractured skull, broken bones, swelling on the brain and much more. They have a nine year old son. This employee's wife is experiencing memory loss and doesn't recognize him and very little of their son. Needless to say, we've all been gutted as a result.

I don't know whether or not he is a believer. And I'm not sure whether this is a poor time to ask or the best time to ask. I try to put myself in his situation. I can't imagine going through something as devastating as that without Christ as my anchor. There are some storms that come our way and we get jostled about, but a storm of this magnitude requires a *"strong and trustworthy anchor for our souls"* (Hebrews 6:19 NLT).

As a believer, we have the ability to surrender the pain and sorrow this life can bring to Jesus. We don't have to carry the weight of our trials alone. But without Jesus, the weight can be so heavy it almost crushes us. I've been there. I've gone through situations where I've carried the heaviness of emotional burdens on my own. I cried out, to myself. And yes, I came through it. But how much easier would it have been if I knew I could cry out to God? How much better would it have been if I knew I had someone that could help me carry the weight *and* bring me peace while I carried it?

But I don't know if this employee knows Jesus. What I do know is, we created a culture of compassion in our workplace that allowed him to see the love of Jesus through us. One of my employees asked if we could come together to provide dinners for this family, in the absence of their wife and mother. The response from our employees was overwhelming. A months worth of meals were scheduled and we began immediately. In addition, my wife, Whitney, packaged lunches for the little boy to make the morning routine a little easier for this family.

The employee was overcome by the outpouring of love and compassion for him and his family. He will have enough on his plate with hospital visits and discussion with doctors as he monitors his wife's progress by the minute. As his work family, we needed to do what we could to alleviate some of the more menial day-to-day activities like cooking.

When you bring Jesus to work and create the Christ-centered foundation in your workplace, and in your life, there's a palpable depth to relationships. Your interactions go from passive to engaged. You go from caring solely if their work is done right and on time to also caring about their passions, hobbies and family.

When you are emotionally connected, the roots of the relationship go deeper and get stronger.

I've noticed there's a reaction time difference between "regular" workplaces and Christ-centered workplaces. For regular workplaces, there's a lag time. There's a gap between situation and response. But for a Christ-centered workplace, the response is immediate. And it begins with prayer. Prayer is always the default position. To be clear, what I am describing isn't a mandatory prayer session for believers and non-believers alike. But, as the Christian leader of your organization, your department or your project, your immediate response should be prayer. Prayer for comfort, strength and healing for the person or people facing adversity. But just as important is prayer for guidance and next steps. How can you, as a Christian, help lift the burden from this employee? For one of my employees, who is a believer, the Holy Spirit lead her to start a meal calendar and ask others to participate. In prayer, be still and listen. The Holy Spirit will guide your steps.

Pain Has a Purpose

I truly believe that compassion in the workplace is like a dedicated focus on the bottom-line. Both are absolutely critical to your organizations success. Because those that we lead are human, we will surely encounter all that the human condition brings. And since most of those we lead will likely be non-believers or those whose lives are not truly Christ-centered, it allows us the opportunity to be the light. As Christians we know that in our weakness, He is strong. But for the non-believers, Christ in us allows us to be strong for them.

When you lead with compassion, you are bringing Jesus to work.

four

Paul Was Saul

Romans 5:8 (NLT)

*"But God showed his great love for us by sending Christ
to die for us while we were still sinners"*

Paul Was Saul

Show of hands...how many of you find it easy to be kind to people that hurt you? Ok, maybe show of hands was the wrong approach. *I can't see you*! What I can see is that my own hand didn't go up in the air. Nice to people that hurt me? No chance. I should say, before coming to Christ there was no chance I would be kind to someone that hurt me or my family and maybe even my friends. And if I'm honest, even after being given the incomprehensible gift of forgiveness, grace and mercy by accepting our Lord Jesus Christ, I still struggle with this on occasion.

As you know, living a Christ-centered life is a daily grind of stumbling and correction. With every decision you make, there is a Christ-like way and a sin-natured way to approach the same issue. Of course, the deeper your faith roots go and the more obedient you become to the Holy Spirit, the easier this dynamic becomes. But it never gets easy.

Every day we are exposed to opportunities to become more Christ-like. I had one just this morning as I was cut off in traffic. Few things will test your religion like being cut off in traffic. I know the old me would have relished moments like that. I'd immediately go all "Top Gun" on the perpetrator. "Top Gun", for those of you unfamiliar, was a movie about fighter jets and fighter pilots released in 1986 featuring Tom Cruise. A movie so inspiring it made me almost want to join the Navy. But God knew, of course, that fighter pilot was much too manly for the likes of me.

But I digress. So, in my youth, I would get cut off in traffic and immediately plan my counter move. Likely cranking up Journey on cassette, I would step on the gas and pull up alongside the infractor, mouthing something less than poetic. Maybe point a finger in their direction and race ahead and cut them off in retaliation. While my car wasn't an F-14 fighter jet, in my mind I could maneuver that car with precision. I was completely oblivious to the obvious dangers of my retaliation, but for a moment, I had won!

Now, having been Holy Spirit filled, I'm just like "oh, that's ok. You likely didn't see me. God's trying to slow me down for a reason..." Ha! I like to think that's how I am now but I know God's got more work to do in me.

It's certainly difficult to be nice to those that hurt us, but I find a void in this world of people just being nice even when someone is nice to them! We see poor customer service everywhere. In fact, great customer service, or kindness, is so rare that we grow accustomed to the absence of kindness as the norm. Books are written about companies that have exceptional customer service because it is so rare.

But the great thing about the lack of kindness in our society is that, as a business, it doesn't take a lot of effort to create a truly memorable experience for your customers. Just having a basic foundation of kindness in your workplace can completely transform your customer experience and their loyalty as a result.

In the industry of entertainment and sports venues, there are thousands of opportunities to be kind just in a three hour game or two hour concert. The guests are coming to us with a desire to escape the daily grind of work and life and get lost in the excitement of a goal or the memories of the song they've been waiting all week to hear.

For venue managers, we have to look at a day-in-the-life of our guests. Let's just take it from the start of their workday and the challenges that can arise on the job. The frustrations we all face. Then, they leave work, maybe go home to welcome the babysitter, get back in the car and get in traffic coming into the event, pay likely too much for parking and by the time they get to our front-line staff, they are ready for an escape. For us, that first inter-action with our guest is critical. It sets the tone for the rest of the evening.

In a pre-event meeting not long ago, I met with all of our ushers and their supervisors. I said, "In the States, we have a saying that helps keep our eyes open for potential dangerous situations. It's 'See Something, Say Something'. If you see something suspicious, like a back-pack on the ground by itself and no obvious owner in sight, say something. Let someone know. Make someone aware of the potential danger. So tonight I want to turn that around. All of us face negativity on a daily basis. The negativity can come from the news, our parents, our sig-nificant others, our co-workers or friends. So tonight, I want to lift people up. If you see an outfit you think is cute, let the guest know. If you See Something, Say Some-thing. If you like someone's hair style, tell them. Let's bring light into the darkness. Let's lift people's spirits up while they are in our presence. If you See Something, Say Something!"

Shortly after that meeting I walked the concourse to make sure we were ready to open doors for the event.

Paul Was Saul

One of my Christian staff came up to me and said "you were preaching up there!" I said "no I wasn't, I was just encouraging everyone". She said, "no, you were preaching!" While I wasn't purposely "preaching", it had the same effect. I titled this book, "Preach Where You Reach" as a result of that encounter. Preaching doesn't only have to come on a Sunday or from the pulpit. We can bring Christ-like qualities and encouragement no matter our audience or location.

As I mentioned, in my entertainment workplace, we had so many opportunities to be kind and really impact the trajectory of a customers experience. If we saw a guest with their hands full of popcorn, nachos and drinks, I encouraged my staff to ask if we can help them carry something to their seat. It is such a small gesture, but in the absence of kindness in the world, these gestures are viewed to be much greater by the guest. Because of the nature of this business, the guests are often trying capture the evening in pictures. We often will see a mom or dad attempting to take a picture of the family at the event and we routinely ask if we can take the picture so they can all be in the photo. Now I understand that these gestures aren't revolutionary, but to the family, they certainly changed their view of our company, and perhaps the world in some small way.

Preach Where You Reach: Bring Your Jesus to Work (*Every*) Day

As leaders in the marketplace, we can't limit our kindness to the confines of your workplace walls. Who do you encounter on any given day or week outside of your office doors? For me, I interacted with politicians, media, tourism departments, city staff, sports tenant ownership/management, other venue operators, vendors, restaurant owners, hotel operators, small business owners and so much more. All of the areas where I reached, afforded me an opportunity to build relationships. And these relationships are birthed from a seed of kindness.

I joined a Christian-based group not long ago that brings together people from various business backgrounds and we discuss our personal lives and business lives through the lens of faith. We have someone that sells apple juice, another that works in construction, another that handles wealth management, another that owns and operates a hotel and more. This diverse group of people are brought together to discuss the Word and how Jesus affects our lives and places of business. I love it. Everyone is coming at the same topic from their respective stage of their walk with Christ. Baptist, Catholic, Pentacostal, non-denominational and more.

Paul Was Saul

One morning, a gentleman who I had not yet met came into the meeting. Everyone clearly knew who he was, except me. He was a short, stocky Italian man in his early 30's. We began, as we do, with prayer and then began our discussion. During the meeting, he mentioned that he wasn't planted in a church. In fact, he stopped going to church. As we continued, he had great insight on our topic and clearly had a fire burning within for Jesus. At the end of the meeting he closed us out in prayer and left for work. The leader of the group pulled me aside. He said "I don't know if you know him, but as you heard, he doesn't go to church now. He lives close to your church and I thought that, if you were comfortable, perhaps you could invite him to church. You can Google him and read about his background. And I understand if you aren't comfortable inviting him. Just thought I'd put it out there".

So, of course, I have to Google the guy! Turns out that he is a member of a notorious crime family (some might say Mafia) and served ten years in prison on a plea bargain related to a murder/"hit". My first reaction was "um, WHAT?!!!!" But what happened next was so God. I heard God say "Paul was Saul". That's all. Three words. Paul was Saul.

For believers, we can understand this reference. Saul was notorious for his persecution and killing of early Jesus followers. He was not a good guy. Until one day, Jesus appeared to Saul in a blinding light as he was traveling from Jerusalem to Damascus and asked "why do you persecute me?" Saul was blinded by the encounter for three days until his sight was restored by Ananias.

The encounter is described in Acts 9:17-18 (NLT) *"17So Ananias went and found Saul. He laid his hands on him and said, "Brother Saul, the Lord Jesus, who appeared to you on the road, has sent me so that you might regain your sight and be filled with the Holy Spirit." 18Instantly something like scales fell from Saul's eyes, and he regained his sight. Then he got up and was baptized."*

Saul is called Paul later in Acts and fourteen of the twenty-seven books in the New Testament are attributed to Paul. You can say he turned his life around after that brief encounter with Jesus.

So after God spoke to me and said those three words, "Paul was Saul", it was clear that this person with a challenging past, but a burning in his heart for Jesus, should be welcomed as a brother in Christ. The next meeting, I invited him to join me at my church and it was clear that the kindness I showed him was not something he was used to receiving. When he attempted to go to churches previously he was faced with judgement and disapproving stares. I was offering him a place where he could come and experience the presence of God without judgement. A place he could get planted and serve. A place of kindness.

I joined this Christian group as a result of my workplace, as a business person in the community, but my influence isn't just reserved to the physical workplace. Because Jesus is in me through the Holy Spirit, wherever I stand is Holy ground. Jesus is with me no matter where my job takes me in the community. There are opportunities to share the kindness of Jesus every single day. This encounter with this gentleman has surely changed me in some way and I believe that God put us together so that God could work through me to not only change his life, but that of his family and generations to come.

When our hearts burn for Jesus, especially when we are babies in our faith, we can overcomplicate what it means to bring Jesus into the workplace or in our various work encounters. We get excited. We want everyone to experience this new found freedom. We want to tell the world. Shout it from the highest point. But unless you work for a church, that approach would likely elicit a call from Human Resources. I'm not suggesting you open your business meetings with prayer or cleverly incorporate scripture into a presentation to clients. You don't need to set up business meetings at the nearest YMCA just in case someone wants to give their life to Christ, there's a pool nearby for baptism. That would just be weird anyway, right?

You start with a seed of kindness. This is so important. I would suggest that this point has much in common with the parable Jesus used when explaining the Kingdom of Heaven. In Matthew 13:31-32 NLT (and Mark and Luke. A parable so nice it's mentioned thrice! I'll use Matthew since it's my middle name...) *"The Kingdom of Heaven is like a mustard seed planted in the field. It is the smallest of all seeds, but it becomes the largest of garden plants; it grows into a tree, and birds come and make nests in its branches."*

Kindness is also like a mustard seed. Something so simple can grow to be the foundation of an amazing business relationship or personal relationship. Just being kind to someone sets the tone for the relationship.

Paul Was Saul

Not long ago, I met the Dean of Business, Media and Entertainment of a local college. I asked to meet with her because I believed that my incredible group of Directors could be impactful to the students in the media and entertainment programs. I thought, perhaps we could be guest lecturers or sit on a panel that could help educate the students in real world scenarios in this crazy business.

When we met, there seemed to be an instant connection. We started talking about concerts she had attended, artists I had met and we just started having a conversation seemingly unrelated to why I asked for the meeting in the first place. She told me one of her favorite artists is Dave Matthews. How her and her husband danced to a Dave Matthews Band song at their wedding. I mentioned having an autographed Dave Matthews guitar in my bedroom and the conversation kept going. When I mentioned I had an upcoming Dixie Chicks concert, she told me how she and her daughters use the Dixie Chicks song "Not Ready To Make Nice" as a rallying anthem and something that bonds them together as mom and daughters. She also told me how her husband went to see Bon Jovi and embarrassed their daughters by playing a pretty mean air guitar. We eventually got to the reason for the meeting and we instantly thought of so many ways that we could partner together moving forward. Later that day, I sent this email:

"It was great meeting you this afternoon. We could have gone on forever talking about concerts. So this just in...I have my suite available for Dixie Chicks on Monday and I wanted to see if you would like to be my guest, along with your daughters if they are available. Even your husband is welcome, but only if he brings his air guitar!! Let me know and I can leave tickets in your name at the box office. My wife will be there with a couple of her friends as well ~ Scott"

She replied:

"Hi Scott,

It was great meeting you as well! I was relaying your awesome stories to everyone when I got home. That is amazing!!! There were some serious hoots in this house when I read your email. We would absolutely love to go! My eldest daughter is still out east finishing up her exams but my husband and daughter would love to come. It's so kind of you...we can't wait!! Thanks and have an awesome night- you certainly made ours!"

Paul Was Saul

You may be thinking, "I really like that 'Wide Open Spaces' song, but what's this have to do with Jesus?' *EVERYTHING!* In Matthew 5:14-16 (NLT) it says *"You are the light of the world - like a city on a hilltop that cannot be hidden. No one lights a lamp and then puts it under a basket. Instead, a lamp is placed on a stand, where it gives light to everyone in the house. In the same way, let your good deeds shine out for all to see, so that everyone will praise your heavenly Father"*.

I love that last part. *"Let your good deeds shine out for all to see, so that everyone will praise your heavenly Father."* It doesn't say "so that everyone will praise you". This isn't about you. It's about what God can do through you to glorify His name. It can begin with just being kind.

One Easter weekend I had Garth Brooks and Trisha Yearwood playing five shows in four days in my arena. My Executive Assistant, Jenn, and her husband Greg are big fans of Garth Brooks. I had teased Jenn for about a year that when Garth came to town, I was going to see if he would sing a little song backstage with her. You see, Jenn is one of our anointed worship leaders at our church and this girl can sing! So, my staff was backstage and I was introducing them to Garth. I got to Jenn. I said,

Preach Where You Reach: Bring Your Jesus to Work (*Every*) Day

"Garth, this is Jenn. She is my Executive Assistant. And I'm gonna be a bit bold right now, but I believe Jenn has an amazing voice and I wanted to see if you would be willing to sing the chorus to 'The River' with her here backstage". Garth looked at Jenn and said "why don't you learn Trisha's song 'How Do I Live' and join me, her and the band on Saturday for soundcheck and we'll do the song together." Jenn was stunned. When Saturday came, I joined Jenn and Greg at soundcheck and awaited Garth to arrive.

Garth came into the arena, gave Jenn and me a big hug like we've been friends for years. He introduced himself to Greg and said "C'mon, let's go". And off to the stage they went.

The band was warming up and Garth, Jenn and Greg were just chatting as everyone prepared. One of Garth's road crew members handed Trisha's microphone to Jenn. Trisha was still in her dressing room as Jenn positioned herself center-stage. The music began and as Jenn started the first line of the song, Garth's eyes, and those of the entire band, lit up with joy. She could clearly sing and the band immediately recognized her talent. While she sang, Trisha came out and sat in the front row and watched.

Paul Was Saul

Jenn's husband Greg was taking pictures as he wiped tears from his face. When Jenn finished the song, Trisha stood up, giving Jenn a standing ovation and said "That was amazing. I can take the night off!"

Garth motioned the band to come to the middle of the stage and they began playing "The River". Greg, also a worship leader in our church, joined the band to sing along with his wife and Garth Brooks. The arena was empty, except for some staff that came to witness this emotional moment. And while the arena chairs were empty, the presence of God filled that arena.

What no one knew at the time, was that the sound engineer had recorded the whole thing from the sound board and Jenn was presented an autographed CD copy from the whole band that evening. This was clearly a moment that Jenn and Greg will cherish for the rest of their lives.

This story isn't about what I did for Jenn, it's about what God did through me out of kindness to Jenn. When you've built relationships on kindness, and you let the Holy Spirit work through you, you can do amazing things for the people that you lead.

What can you do, out of kindness, for an employee, a co-worker, a client or a customer? It's amazing what can come from a mustard seed.

When you lead with kindness, you are bringing Jesus to work.

five

Are We Getting New Uniforms?!

3 John 2 (ESV)

"Beloved, I pray that all may go well with you and that you may be in good health, as it goes well with your soul"

Are We Getting New Uniforms?

Have you ever encountered a group of people that have been so beat down or repressed that even when you come to deliver them from that, they're skeptical and give you attitude? Oh, I have. I've seen this in various forms, from dysfunctional, destructive personal relationships to cities that have been the brunt of jokes for so long. After a while, they start to own it.

As I mentioned in Chapter two, before we officially took over management of our venues in Hamilton, my Directors and I met with the part-time staff. What started out as a positive, uplifting meeting to discuss who we were, how we operate and what they could expect from this exciting new chapter in our lives quickly turned into a forum for the part-time employees to let out all the emotion that had built up for years. The flood gates opened and in poured the deluge.

"Are we gonna have more shows?" one lady asked. One gentleman in a wheelchair said "I always get stuck in the same spot. I'd love to see more of the building and work in other areas. I don't like being in the same location every single show!" It seemed with every new question there was an elevated frustration. Once one employee opened up, more and more felt comfortable expressing some of their dissatisfaction with how things had been run previously.

Are we getting new uniforms?!" one woman asked with strong irritation on her breath. "Absolutely!" I said. "But first, we'd want to talk to you about what you'd like to wear. What makes sense for the arena versus the theatre. We'd want your input before we just order uniforms." Well you would have thought Jesus himself had just walked up behind me based on the looks I got. They seemed stunned. Their faces seemed to say "You want our opinion?! We haven't had that before."

The part-time staff felt disrespected, historically. They felt like they hadn't been heard. They felt like they hadn't had a voice. And here was some unfamiliar guy from the States saying he wanted to hear them. It was unfamiliar territory for them. And it was the beginning of the healing.

When we think of healing, our minds immediately go to obvious sickness. We get a cut, it heals in a week. We break a bone, it heals in four to six weeks and so on. I know this very well. As a child, I spent many days in doctor's offices and hospital rooms from various injuries.

Are We Getting New Uniforms?

In no particular order...I broke my wrist from an inside pitch I couldn't escape; had my head split open with a hammer (with friends like these...); broke my kneecap slipping on ice; had a window slam down on my thumb and split it open; sprained both knees at the same time by jumping into a pool; was shot by a neighbor extremely close to my eye with a BB gun; and many other injuries too numerous to mention. My poor mother. If these injuries happened today, I'm sure I would have been removed from my home and placed into protective care. I just was one of those kids. When I played sports, I didn't care about my body, I cared about the play. I see this now in my son and it drives me crazy. But I am incredibly grateful for the nurses and doctors and their ability to help me heal.

When we think of healing in the Bible, we think of Jesus healing lepers or making the blind see again. We think of the paralyzed man that was lowered from the roof, described in Luke 5, who gets up to walk. We think of the story of the women with bleeding issues that touched the edge of a garment Jesus wore and her bleeding issues she had endured for twelve years immediately ceased. All of these examples are obvious signs of healing. But I want you to know that, as a leader in the workplace, you too can bring healing to those you lead.

Most, if not all, of us have experienced something in our lives that has had a lasting negative impact on us. We've been scarred, emotionally. Our emotional injuries can be as simple as having been stifled in our jobs by a boss that didn't let us truly realize our potential to verbal abuse by a parent to molestation by a family member or neighbor. We could have gone through a difficult custody fight or divorce. We could have had a child or spouse die. Everyone's pain is different and how everyone handles pain is equally different. What can seem trivial to one person has the ability to be a decade long pain for another. As I've mentioned before, all of this emotional hurt doesn't get checked at the door when we come to work.

As a disciple of Christ in the workplace, we know that God can work through us to bring healing to those we lead. When we incorporate Christ-like attributes in the workplace, like compassion and kindness, we have the ability to transform an employee's or co-worker's life. At the very least, we have the ability to bring healing in the workplace.

Are We Getting New Uniforms?

The part-time staff I mentioned earlier is such an example. During that 'town hall" with the employees, I listened. I heard their pain. I heard their sadness. And I offered hope. We were going to go in a new direction, after all, that's why we were brought in to manage the venues. While I knew the changes ahead were going to be difficult for some of the staff, as change is never easy, I encouraged them to believe in us. I encouraged them to trust that we were going to address the issues and make the workplace a place of joy.

Over the first year, we implemented policies and procedures that not everyone liked but were best for the health of the organization and ultimately best for the employees in our care. What was interesting to watch was, all of the employees that were most vocal, most frustrated, stayed with us. Those that thought things were pretty good before we got there ended up leaving. I'm reminded of a Pastor that once said "Don't worry about those that leave you. They can't go where you're going!"

A number of months into our tenure at these venues, one of the employees that was most frustrated in the beginning stopped me as I walked the concourse before an event. He said, "I just want to tell you that I am so grateful that you came here. I have never been happier at work. You talk to us. You care about us. You listen to us. You have done an outstanding job and I just wanted you to know." I gave him a high five and I thanked him. As I walked away, I started to get emotional. What a transformation. He was miserable at work and now he tells me he's never been happier. He had emotional scars. But God...

Healing.

I'm terrible with math. Well, I shouldn't say terrible, but out of all the areas I oversee on any given day, finance is where I need the most help. I could certainly work my way around the budget or work up artist offers and profit/loss analysis but there are some finance functions where I just needed someone smarter than me. When I came to Hamilton, I was basically told who my Director of Finance was going to be. I didn't know her, had never met her. Knowing this is the one area I really needed someone strong, I was cautiously optimistic. It was clear to me from the beginning that this person was exactly who I needed in such a role. I was immediately comfortable with her and I looked to her daily for financial advice and forecasting.

Are We Getting New Uniforms?

It was likely a year into our work relationship, during a one on one meeting, that she opened up to me. She let me know that at her previous facility, the General Manager had a finance background. As a result, he would often do the work that she felt was her work. Now, her former boss didn't do this with any ill-intent. He just happened to be proficient in finance and was able to create a quick financial analysis and decide direction on his own. "But since coming here", she said "I've been able to really grow in my role as a Director of Finance. You've given me the autonomy and you've trusted in me and that has allowed me to flourish here. I am so much happier. I wasn't sure about moving to Hamilton, but this was clearly a move I needed. So, thank you." Her former colleagues who had worked with her in the other facility noticed a dramatic change in her attitude and outlook. There had been a transformation.

Healing.

Hamilton, as a city, has been scarred. Locals would likely be too proud to admit it, but I see it on their faces and in their actions. Hamilton has been the brunt of jokes for years. Its manufacturing roots and smoke stacks were comedic fodder for those living in Toronto and surrounding communities. I'm reminded of Cleveland.

For much of my adult life, Cleveland had the reputation as the "arm pit" of the States. I mean, the Cuyahoga River in Cleveland actually caught on fire! The river!! *Water caught fire!* The late, great comedian Bob Hope has been credited with saying if he had one brother in a penitentiary and another brother in Cleveland, he'd visit the penitentiary first. Of course, Cleveland is now an amazing city that has undergone a dramatic transformation and has become the envy and example of many cities across North America looking for reinvention.

Hamilton, for so long, has been the punchline. And while the city is undergoing its own transformation, including an ironic influx of Torontonians, the emotional scars remain. I saw these scars when I was fortunate to secure a Paul McCartney date for our arena. Hamiltonians were shocked. They would say, "I can't believe Paul McCartney is coming to Hamilton. I mean, it's Hamilton!" Others would say "I can see McCartney playing Toronto, but this is Hamilton!"

I remember being asked to be on a radio show to discuss the Paul McCartney show. The host said "Scott, this is an amazing show for Hamilton. Why do you think McCartney chose to play Hamilton?" I said, "why wouldn't he? Hamilton is an amazing city, with wonderful people. I think we need to start telling ourselves that. We need to start believing in ourselves." But that has been a foreign concept for so many locals. Sometimes it takes someone from the outside to remind us just how special our city is. Outsiders tend to focus on the positive in a city. Locals tend to focus on the negative. I don't think Hamilton is unique in that regard, but it's certainly something that I've witnessed having lived in this great city.

A couple years ago, I was invited to participate on a panel to discuss Hamilton as a Music City. This Chamber of Commerce-sponsored event brought various people from the music industry together, as well as a full theatre of interested guests from the community. During the panel, I mentioned this very subject. In my opinion, Hamilton has been beaten down for so long that, much like an abusive relationship, we begin to own what is said about us. We start to believe the lies. We begin to view ourselves as others view us.

After the panel concluded, a number of people approached me and said "you did a great job. You were saying exactly what we needed to hear". Again, this isn't me. This is God through me. I'm just a vessel. But I am grateful that God chose me to help unite this city and lift its collective head a bit higher. Hamilton needs to believe that, like us, it is fearfully and wonderfully made. I've had opportunities, through my position at work, to influence and impact this extraordinary city. I have the ability to preach where I reach and help heal a broken city.

In my entertainment venues, I had three employees that went to the same church in which I'm planted. One of our dearest friends from our church, Dean, had gone into the hospital and suffered cardiac arrest on multiple occasions while there. Just when things appeared to be looking up, I got a call that Dean went into cardiac arrest again and he was fighting for his life. Without hesitation, I called the employees that go to our church into my office and closed the door. I explained what was happening and we immediately began to pray for supernatural healing. We prayed for his wife and kids. We prayed for the doctors and nurses as they worked to save Dean's life. We went to war with whatever was coming against our friend. We know that prayer can change outcomes. We know that the supernatural can work miracles that leaves doctors wondering how such healing could ever take place. We stand firm in our faith and what that faith and prayer can do. Dean was brought back to life on that day. He had been brought back to life several times. His ribs broken from so many compressions. Later we prayed that God's will be done. God took Dean home a day or two later.

While we came together in prayer for healing for Dean, moments like that helped me see that sometimes the prayers for healing help us heal. Experiencing the death of a close friend is painful, but we saw God answer our prayers. That moment in the workplace, through prayer, helped us prepare for the death that was to come. Just having that communion with our Father in Heaven helped us heal from the pain of separation from such an amazing man.

If I am to write a truly transparent book, I have to also give an example of when I've failed. Like all of us, I continue to be a work in progress. I'm on a journey to be more Christ-like and I am reminded, at times, that this is a lifelong journey and I will fail along the way.

I had two of my employees that looked to restructure their department. I was fully supportive. Both of these employees are outstanding and surely deserved the growth they were trying to achieve in this restructure.

Preach Where You Reach: Bring Your Jesus to Work (*Every*) Day

The concept had been discussed with our corporate office and we felt like we were in a good position to move forward. We even announced the restructuring at a staff meeting to cheers and congratulations. A few months went by and there was a some concern from our corporate office about the new direction. Executives came to meet with me and the employees to discuss further. After detailed discussion, it was determined that we couldn't move forward with the restructuring at this time. The reasoning was sound and well thought out. We understood, but the wind was completely taken out of the sails of these two employees. As I left the meeting with the two employees to walk back to our offices. I could see they were deflated and I chose to not saying anything in that moment, as we walked back to the office. We walked back in complete silence.

The next day, the employees asked to meet with me. When we sat down, they had a number of things they wanted to talk about but one thing stood out among them all. My silence. They were hurt. I didn't comfort them in their sadness and they know that's not like me. I told them that I purposely chose to stay silent because I felt like the disappointing meeting just needed to sink in instead of me being a cheerleader and encourager. But that's not what they needed in that moment. That's not what they needed from me to heal from the disappointment. So my silence actually created another scar for them.

In Lamentations 3:22-23 (NLT) it says *"The faithful love of the Lord never ends. His mercies never cease. Great is His faithfulness; His mercies begin afresh each morning."* I am reminded of this when I fail. I get a restart the next day and I can ask the Holy Spirit to guide my footsteps, guide my words and actions. I will fail. You will fail. But with forgiveness, prayer and surrender, we get a fresh start every day to bring Christ into the workplace.

Healing comes in many forms because hurt comes in many forms. Healing can come from something as simple as listening. Healing can come from allowing someone to flourish in their job duties. Healing can come from lifting others up above their past, their reputation or their own misconceptions of themselves. Healing can come from prayer.

Healing isn't just for those in the medical field. Healing can come from accountants, construction workers, bank tellers and entertainment executives. Healing can come from you. Let the Holy Spirit guide you. Be obedient. See lives transformed.

When you lead with healing, you are bringing Jesus to work.

six

No Palm Trees in Hamilton

Proverbs 3:13-18 (NLT)

13"*Joyful is the person who finds wisdom, the one who gains understanding.*
14 *For wisdom is more profitable than silver, and her wages are better than gold.*
15 *Wisdom is more precious than rubies; nothing you desire can compare with her.* **16** *She offers you long life in her right hand, and riches and honor in her left.*
17 *She will guide you down delightful paths; all her ways are satisfying.* **18** *Wisdom is a tree of life to those who embrace her; happy are those who hold her tightly*".

No Palm Trees in Hamilton

I am a beach fanatic. Seriously. I absolutely *love* the beach. I know the Bible gives us a vision of what heaven will be like in Revelation. It speaks of streets of gold and walls of jasper. But if I'm being honest, I just hope heaven is a white sand beach with beautiful turquoise water. I'm not a big fan of gold anyway. Give me a Caribbean beach and a sunny day and I'm in heaven. At least heaven on earth. Maybe throw in a banana daiquiri for good measure.

I have a music playlist called "Beach". It's mostly made up of Kenny Chesney's more beach-influenced songs but it can put me right on the beach, mentally, even through the rough Canadian winters. This is where I am at peace. Besides church, this is where I feel most connected to God. There's a calm, a tranquility. The beach is where I can be still and just sit at the feet of Jesus.

Now picture this conversation. My wife and I are living in Cleveland and I say, "Hey, babe - I have an opportunity to move to the Bahamas with my company! Can you believe it? We've gotta do this. This is a dream opportunity. I am beyond excited! We wake up each day and guess what we're doing? Living in the Bahamas!!"

Now, my wife loves the beach, as well, but as a good wife and mother of our children should do, she tried to slow me down a bit. Help me take a breather. Maybe let it marinate a bit. I tell her all about the opportunity and I am absolutely pumped. There is absolutely no doubt where we're moving. I immediately went into research mode. What's housing like, where would the kids go to school, how is crime, how expensive are utilities and groceries? I even got a realtor. My real estate agent began sending me pictures of home options. I'd show my wife pictures of these amazing houses with beautiful, crystal-clear water right outside the master bedroom. You have to understand, this is the perfect job for me.

During this time, there was also an opportunity in Hamilton, Ontario. Sure the arena in Hamilton did some pretty amazing concerts, *but this was the Bahamas!* But then the Bahamas possibility did what things in the Bahamas do, it slowed down. There was an election that put the entire job possibility in jeopardy. All the while, I was doing my due diligence on Hamilton. Same research. Housing, crime, schools, etc. As much as I wanted the Bahamas, deep down something didn't feel quite right. My realtor sent me more information. In the Bahamas, it was suggested that we live in a gated community and send the kids to private school. My wife and I decided we needed to sit down and really talk this through.

After some careful consideration, we decided we had to make a move that was best for our family as a whole. In the Bahamas, we would have to live in a gated community with other mostly "well-to-do" white people and send our kids to private schools while the rest of the islands population was on the other side of the gates. But, if we moved to Hamilton, we could give our kids an international experience without too much culture shock. In the end, we decided to move the family to Hamilton, *where there isn't a single palm tree*! Do I sound bitter?

Looking back on that time now makes me laugh. We actually thought we were making the decision. Meanwhile, God was orchestrating the entire thing. I know this because my wife, my children and I all got saved when we came to Hamilton. I was always supposed to come to Hamilton, I just needed some God-infused wisdom to get me there.

Wisdom is a funny thing. We think we have so much of it, especially as we get older. We may know more things, but there's a difference between knowledge and wisdom. In Proverbs 3:7-8 (NLT) it says *"Don't be impressed with your own wisdom. Instead, fear the Lord and turn away from evil. Then you will have healing for your body and strength for your bones."* I encourage you to read Proverbs thoroughly. It's just such a great resource for how to live your life with Godly wisdom.

There will surely be times when you will impart wisdom into someone you lead in the workplace. But there will also be times when you need to hear wisdom as well. And for some of us, me included, it takes longer to get to clarity on an issue because we don't seek wisdom soon enough.

Matt, a close friend of mine who is also a Christian, came to me about a year ago, after beginning a new position within his company. His new position brought added responsibility along with added salary, but it also brought a change in boss. While they may have had a similar end goal, a healthy bottom line, they had very different ways of achieving that goal. Matt and his new boss viewed the same task in reverse order. His boss saw numbers first, people second. Matt saw people first, numbers second. The fact that my friend put numbers second doesn't mean he didn't care about the numbers. But in his previous position, he found that by caring about the people, it was easier to achieve the numbers.

No Palm Trees in Hamilton

Needless to say, the approaches were different and as a result, there was a tension in the relationship. Additionally, Matt had put up a figurative wall and had difficulty receiving what his boss would say to him. Matt reached out to me and asked for advice.

Have you ever prayed negative prayers? Prayers that are not life-giving? I mean, they seem like the right thing to pray at the time, but they lack Biblical wisdom. That's what Matt was doing. He was praying that his boss would be removed from his division of the company. He prayed that he would be free from his authority. He was praying negative. And then I shared with him Matthew 5:44 (NLT) *"But I say, love your enemies! Pray for those who persecute you!"* Matt was praying *against* his boss, but the Bible says to pray *for*. That was exactly the paradigm shift he needed. And so he began to pray life into this man. Matt prayed that he would honor his boss, that his boss would see Christ in and through him. He prayed that his boss' heart would turn from a harsh numbers only focus and instead see the employees as people rather than just a means to an end. He prayed that the walls he had built up making communications even more difficult, would fall. Matt prayed that the Holy Spirit would guide him in their interactions. And through this type of prayer, Matt got a revelation.

I suggested Matt picture a sifter, or sieve, in his head. You know, the tool you use to sort the things you want from the unwanted material. I told him to envision taking what his boss would say and applying a sifter to it. The delivery of what his boss would say was challenging to him at times. The tone or attitude of what was being said would blind Matt to the truth that was being said. After applying this approach, Matt learned to strip away the delivery and focus on the truth. Regardless of how his boss was saying something, his intentions were usually good. Matt just needed to start choosing to hear the substance through the noise of poor delivery.

During this time I also came across more wisdom in the Bible, found in Romans 13:1 (NLT), *"Everyone must submit to governing authorities. For all authority comes from God, and those in positions of authority have been placed there by God."* Just as God had placed Matt in a position of authority over those he leads, Matt's boss had also been placed in his position of authority. There is something Matt had to learn from him, or something his boss had to learn from Matt. I encouraged Matt to read Romans 13:1 for further clarity. After reading the Word and taking my advice, my friend began to pray that he would learn from his boss what he needed to learn. As a result of this biblical wisdom, Matt's relationship has changed dramatically with his boss. They remain very different. Their approaches remain almost polar opposite. But Matt's soul is at peace because of what the Bible continues to teach him. Biblical wisdom, when obeyed, delivers freedom.

At one point, I had one of my managers considering a move within our company. This young man had a desire and passion to develop in new areas of our organization, gaining knowledge and personal growth. And while I would have been disappointed, selfishly, to see him leave our venues, I would've certainly supported his decision to do so. This new position would mean $20,000 increase in pay and a significant title change as well. On the surface, it seemed like a good move. But he had some hesitation and asked if he could speak to me regarding the opportunity.

We met one night during a hockey game. We sat down in a less crowded section of the arena, watched the game and caught up on the opportunity that was before him. He asked my opinion on the position and facility. After talking about similar opportunities that I had been presented over my career and how I decided what to do, I could tell he needed further clarity. I asked if I could offer an opinion, not as the General Manager but as a friend. Hungry for anything that would help point him in the right direction, he said "Absolutely".

I said "As a man of faith, I've learned to let the Holy Spirit guide me. I've thought of walking away from my position several times since moving to Hamilton. I haven't done that for two reasons. First, I believe that until God closes the door where you are, you don't look for a new open door. Secondly, I believe that if you have any unease or hesitation in your 'gut', the opportunity is not from God. Anything that comes from God will be surrounded by peace". We spent a little more time talking and went back to work. A week or so later, he decided not to take the job. He had to get to that decision on his own, but I believe our faith discussion played a role, however small.

When you are Holy Spirit filled and you have a healthy diet of consuming the Word, either through reading the Bible, listening to your favorite pastor deliver a message or through various podcasts, God will use that diet to feed those that you lead, through you. You have to consume the Word in order to impart wisdom into other's lives. If you don't receive the Word, you can't deliver the Word. You can't deliver a pizza unless you have a pizza to deliver, right? Pizza sounds amazing right now! Just a little pepperoni and bacon. I keep it simple.

While it may seem like I am so wisdom-filled that I just hand it out like presents at Christmas, I've been a slow learner. I can still see the headline in the local Ocean City, Maryland newspaper, "Fireworks Cause Fireworks!". I was the Director of Special Events for the Town of Ocean City overseeing events such as concerts on the beach, festivals, celebrity golf tournaments and our annual fireworks display. I'm in my early twenties at that time and I think the biggest firework I had ever handled up to that point was a sparkler. I worked closely with the three biggest firework companies and received bids from each. I poured over the respective bids and compared size of shells and overall costs to determine who I believe should be awarded the opportunity to present our highly anticipated and much-loved annual fireworks extravaganza.

As it was standard protocol for procuring any vendor of this magnitude, I went before the Mayor and City Council to present the case. I had never presented in front of a Mayor and City Council before, and while I was nervous, I felt very confident in my conclusion. After all, I had done my due diligence and I would be recommending the fireworks display that would give us the most bang for the buck, literally.

After my presentation and recommendation, the Mayor took exception. "From what I can see, there are too many small shells. I'd like to see a show with bigger shells", he said. "I can do that", I said, "but the show you want to see will last about five minutes. I've carefully balanced the small shells and the larger shells in order to give us a longer show that still engages our visitors and residents." The Mayor continued on "I just think we need bigger shells, that's what the people want to see." We went back and forth for a bit until I was instructed by council to go back and try to incorporate a few more big shells without compromising the length, if at all possible. After the council session had concluded for the evening, the City Manager walked over to me. He said "I wanted to take a rubber band and shoot you in the crotch just to get you to sit down and shut up".

Funny to think that a threatened rubber band to the crotch can impart wisdom, but it did. I learned valuable

No Palm Trees in Hamilton

lessons in that council meeting. A lesson of respect. A lesson of knowing your audience. A lesson of knowing when to speak and when to bite your tongue. But I had an arrogance about me that, had it not been checked, could have derailed my career. The City Manager, who is still a friend to this day, wasn't preaching from Proverbs, but he might as well have been.

Proverbs 21:23 ESV
"Whoever keeps his mouth and his tongue keeps himself out of trouble".

Proverbs 15:1 ESV
"A soft answer turns away wrath, but a harsh word stirs up anger".

Proverbs 12:18 ESV
"There is one whose rash words are like sword thrusts, but the tongue of the wise brings healing".

I was able to add some additional larger shells, after sharing the newspaper headline with our fireworks provider. The show was fantastic and I walked away a little wiser.

Preach Where You Reach: Bring Your Jesus to Work (*Every)* Day

As a leader, you will encounter some new hires that are ready to tackle the world. They will be full of textbook knowledge and anxious to make a difference. It will be your responsibility to harness that excitement and point it in the right direction. In addition, you will also have more seasoned employees that make poor decisions. As a Christian leader, imparting biblical wisdom must be incorporated into your coaching and mentoring as well as your disciplinary conversations. It will be important that you have not only the biblical knowledge, but discernment on how to convey the heart of Jesus without violating corporate policy.

As believers, we have to have the wisdom to know how to balance our faith and our work. In a secular workplace, you have to be careful that you aren't violating any company policies regarding religion in the workplace. I would never suggest otherwise. I truly believe that when you are filled with the Holy Spirit and you consume a healthy diet of the Word of God, you will be guided in what to say and what *not* to say; when to say something and when *not* to say something.

No Palm Trees in Hamilton

When faced with big decisions or difficult situations at work, I encourage you to seek wisdom from the Bible, certainly, but I would also suggest speaking to your church leadership. Surely, as Christian leader in the workplace, you should be imparting wisdom to those you lead, but you have to get filled up as well. Does your thinking on a specific situation align with the Word? Is there agreement among those you trust to speak Godly wisdom into your life? At my church, we often go to our pastors if there is a major decision to be made in our personal lives. Not because it's mandated by them, but because it just makes sense. I trust my pastors. They are much more versed in the Word and the context of the Word than I am. If I have a major decision to make at work, you can bet that I would include them to help guide my decision making.

Day in and day out, my compass, my guide is Proverbs. This powerful book of the Bible will help guide you in moments of crisis, challenges, adversity and general living. Ultimately, all wisdom comes from having a relationship with God the Father. And like any father and child relationship, you'd be well served to listen to the words of the Father.

Preach Where You Reach: Bring Your Jesus to Work (*Every*) Day

Proverbs 8:1-11 (NLT)

1"Listen as Wisdom calls out! Hear as understanding raises her voice! 2On the hilltop along the road, she takes her stand at the crossroads. 3By the gates at the entrance to the town, on the road leading in, she cries aloud, 4"I call to you, to all of you! I raise my voice to all people. 5You simple people, use good judgment. You foolish people, show some understanding. 6Listen to me For I have important things to tell you. Everything I say is right, 7for I speak the truth and detest every kind of deception. 8My advice is wholesome. There is nothing devious or crooked in it. 9My words are plain to anyone with understanding, clear to those with knowledge. 10Choose my instruction rather than silver, and knowledge rather than pure gold. 11For wisdom is far more valuable than rubies. Nothing you desire can compare with it".

When you lead with wisdom, you are bringing Jesus to work.

seven

The 'Bird and Ryan Gosling

John 13:23 (NLT)

"The disciple Jesus loved was sitting next to Jesus at the table"

The 'Bird and Ryan Gosling

It was a 1976 Pontiac Firebird. It was owned by my best friend, Donnie, and I was parked next to it in my 1976 Ford Granada. It was our senior year of high school. Before you start doing the math, the year was not 1976, it was actually 1985 and we were on top of the world. Well, actually we were at our schools "Activity Night", which was an event that split our high school gym into halves. One half was sports, mainly basketball, and the other side was a dance club with a DJ. I usually stayed on the dance side, because, well, I've got moves! On this particular night, as the event was coming to a close, I went out to my car with my girlfriend. We got in the car, I put my car in reverse and stepped on the gas. For some reason I didn't put my hands on the wheel as I went backwards at what seemed to be a very high rate of speed. My front passenger-side quarter panel introduced itself to the back, driver-side quarter panel of Donnie's Firebird. And time stood still.

As Donnie was summoned to the scene by his brother, I awaited the fireworks that would surely go off upon his arrival. And they did. *He really loved that car!* But all these years later, what could have been a friendship ending incident among high school kids has become an opportunity for a great laugh and memory.

Preach Where You Reach: Bring Your Jesus to Work (*Every)* Day

I met Donnie when I moved to a new city and new school when I was in eighth grade. Anyone who's ever gone through eighth grade surely understands that it's not necessarily the best year to move somewhere new. Establishing new friendships can be tough. After all, many of these kids have been friends since Kindergarten! And while I don't remember the exact thing that drew Donnie and I together, despite living in different cities and countries, we've never strayed from one another. Next to my wife, he is literally my best friend. And we all have them. That one best friend that you've fought with, cried with, laughed with and could never forget. Even Jesus had a best friend, or so the Bible seems to suggest. While Jesus was certainly close with Peter and James, only one disciple is called "the one who Jesus loved." That disciple was John. We know this because John tells us! At the Last Supper, described in John 13:21-25 (NLT), it reads *21Now Jesus was deeply troubled, and he exclaimed, "I tell you the truth, one of you will betray me!" 22The disciples looked at each other, wondering whom he could mean. 23The disciple Jesus loved was sitting next to Jesus at the table. 24Simon Peter motioned to him to ask, "Who's he talking about?" 25So that disciple leaned over to Jesus and asked, "Lord, who is it?"*

The 'Bird and Ryan Gosling

Of course, we know that Judas was the betrayer, but I find it most interesting how John, who wrote this, refers to himself. He could have said "I was sitting next to Jesus at the table", but he seems to want to make it very clear that he and Jesus were extremely close friends. In fact, we see further evidence in the Bible to suggest this close friendship. John was witness to some of the greatest miracles by Jesus; John, along with Peter and James, were brought to a high mountain to pray and witnessed the Transfiguration of Jesus; John was entrusted with caring for Mary, mother of Jesus, by Jesus as He hung on the cross and John was given the Book of Revelation by Jesus. In fact, John was the only disciple present at the crucifixion of Christ. Now that's friendship!

We know, from the Bible, that Jesus had other important, deep-rooted relationships with others as well. Even beyond the twelve disciples, Jesus had meaningful relationships. One of these friendships was a man named Lazarus. You may be familiar with his sisters, Mary and Martha and the story told in Luke, chapter ten. Jesus came to their house for dinner. OK, stop right there. Can you just imagine that? Jesus is gonna just come over to *your* house for dinner. I tidy up the house for the people that come to actually *clean my house*! But this is *Jesus!* I would likely want to buy all new furniture for this visit. Let's be honest, new dishes, new glassware and you might as well give the dog a bath.

So, as it's explained in Luke, Jesus comes over and Martha is just hustlin' and bustlin'. She's preparing the meal, tidying up the place and then there's Mary. Mary is just relaxing at the feet of Jesus, just soaking in the moment. And Martha is getting mad. She's doing all the work! And Martha says to Jesus, *"Lord, doesn't it seem unfair to you that my sister just sits here while I do all the work? Tell her to come and help me."* Jesus replies *"My dear Martha, you are worried and upset over all these details!"* In the Message version, it says Jesus replied *"Martha, dear Martha, you're fussing far too much and getting yourself worked up over nothing. One thing only is essential, and Mary has chosen it—it's the main course, and won't be taken from her."* In other words, understand what is important. Let's just have a relationship. Those other things aren't important. Certainly not more important than a real relationship with Jesus. But the relationship among Mary, Martha, Lazarus and Jesus takes what appears to be a tragic turn. In John 11:3-7 (NLT) it says, *"So the two sisters sent a message to*

The 'Bird and Ryan Gosling

Jesus telling him, "Lord, your dear friend is very sick." *The Bible says "But when Jesus heard about it he said,* *"Lazarus's sickness will not end in death. No, it hap-* *pened for the glory of God so that the Son of God will re-* *ceive glory from this." **5***So although Jesus loved Martha,* *Mary, and Lazarus, **6** he stayed where he was for the* *next two days. **7** Finally, he said to his disciples, "Let's go* *back to Judea."*

So Jesus goes back to Judea, knowing full well that while Lazarus, his friend, was physically dead, for all intents and purposes, Jesus was about to bring him back to life for the Glory of God. Of course Mary and Martha were distraught over the death of their brother and they were hurting, as we all would be if our brother had passed away. What I love about this story in John is that we see both the Divine and the human Jesus displayed.

Mary had run to Jesus and fell at his feet. John 11:33-36 (NLT) continues the scene."***33** When Jesus saw her* *weeping and saw the other people wailing with her, a* *deep anger welled up within him, and he was deeply* *troubled. **34** "Where have you put him?" he asked them.* *They told him, "Lord, come and see." **35** Then Jesus* *wept. 36 The people who were standing nearby said, "See how much he loved him!"*

Jesus wept! I mean, I cry watching The Notebook (don't pretend you didn't!), but this is Jesus. His heart was breaking for Mary and Martha even though he knew Lazarus was about to be brought to life.

Relationships are absolutely critical in our workplaces. I know what it's like to weep because of adversity in an employee's life. I've shed tears over an employee's parent attempting suicide. I've wept when an employee's dog had to have a leg amputated because of cancer. And the tears are shed because of the deep relationships I've created. But relationships don't always have to be viewed through the lens of grief or sadness. Relationships build businesses. Relationships build client lists and portfolios. Relationships, especially outside of your employees, help build your name and reputation in your town or city.

Relationships take effort, however. They may be birthed through a seed of kindness, but they have to be watered with intent. You have to actively keep the relationship alive.

The 'Bird and Ryan Gosling

Have you ever dreamed of stumbling upon a magic lamp? You know the kind, with a genie inside that grants you three wishes. I know I have. Of course that was BC, "Before Christ", so don't judge me.

I can't remember exactly what I thought I'd wish for but I think everyone's wishes tend to start with either a wish for more wishes or a wish for a million dollars. The million dollar wish cracks me up though. We say it because we want to be a "millionaire", but as soon as we spend a dollar, we're out of that club. How about asking for $800 million?

Sidebar, I think we treat our prayers the same way. Instead of praying for something so huge only God could execute it, we pray small. A promotion, a raise. I encourage you, when calling on God, pray huge prayers!

I believe many of us treat our relationship with God like a genie in a bottle, or magic lamp. When we have a need or a desire, we call out for God in prayer, but otherwise we have no real relationship. I've met people that say they are Christians. They accept Jesus Christ as their Lord and Saviour, but that's where it ends. They don't open a Bible, they aren't planted or serving in a church. In fact, many don't go to a church at all. They may know of God, but there's no relationship there. And even in the absence of the relationship, they reach out to God and say "hey God, can you do me a favor? Can you take away this cancer? Can you make my wife love me again? Can you help my daughter get into that university?"

In your workplace, as with God, that won't work. You can't call on someone for something when you haven't established a relationship. Try it in your personal life. Go to your local grocery store and throw your items up there on the conveyor with someone else's groceries and see how inclined they are to pay for them for you. They won't bless you because they don't know you. While I'm fairly certain the customer ahead of you won't pay for your groceries, I'd love to see their expression.

In our church, like many churches, we have a youth group. Our youth ministry is called Poema Youth. Most of the children in our youth ministry come from difficult home-life situations, poverty, abuse and general neglect. Every week we bus kids in from all over the city and let them know they are loved by God and by us. We let them

The 'Bird and Ryan Gosling

experience what family can be and help them break cycles of generational sin in their families. Like most youth groups, we look for ways to raise money to allow that ministry to continue to flourish and change lives. One way we look to raise money is through an annual golf scramble.

Because I had worked very hard to establish authentic relationships through my workplace, I was able to call on these relationships to help me drive fundraising for this very important personal initiative. The workplace relationships I'd invested in and grown allowed me to do work for the Kingdom. Because I continued to pour into these relationships year round, it was easier to call on them when this annual event rolled around each spring.

Whether it was through getting buses cheaper than we were previously paying or asking fellow business people to sponsor a golf hole, I was able to raise thousands of dollars for our youth ministry. This is another great Preach Where You Reach example. Many, if not most, of those that I called on to help me with the golf scramble fundraiser are not obvious believers. In fact, some that helped me and our church, would consider themselves athiests. But because I had established a relationship with them, they were happy to help me and our church raise money for our youth ministry. These relationships helped build God's Kingdom. Never think that you can't use your position at work to build God's Kingdom. But always remember, it's not about the position, it's about the relationships you build.

When I moved to Hamilton, one of the first things I did was reach out to the various city councillors. In my position, I sometimes had to interact with and seek approval from the councillors. But before I ever went before them to ask for something, I wanted to have a relationship with them. I wanted to introduce myself, but I also wanted to know what was important to them as a city representative. Many took me up on my invitation to meet and we had great conversations. I'm happy to say that those that agreed to get together with me a few years ago continued to be the one's with whom I had the strongest relationships.

Our church was built on prayer. It has been, and continues to be, an extremely important part of our DNA. One evening, we discussed really ramping up our prayers for the city. We could do generic prayer for the city, but we want to pray specific prayers. Like we see in Mark

The 'Bird and Ryan Gosling

10:46-52 (NLT), Jesus summons a blind beggar that had been calling out to him and asks him *"What do you want me to do for you?"* The blind man said *"That I might see again".* *Jesus said to him, "Go your way. Your faith has made you well."* And the blind man received his sight immediately. Jesus asked for specifics and the beggar's specific prayer was answered.

As a small group from our church gathered one night to discuss this initiative, it was decided that we would look to each political ward, or area, of the city and find out what specific needs they had for prayer. Hamilton is made up of fifteen wards, each represented by a city council member. I volunteered to reach out to all the council members to get their specifics for their wards, as they would surely know the needs better than any of us.

A couple of days later, I reached out to each city council member explaining that separate from my "day job", I was passionately active in my church. I asked each of them for specific needs in their wards that could benefit from a strong faith and prayer infusion. And the answers came pouring in. Many were the same - crime, poverty, senior citizens and the like. I even had one councillor ask for prayers for herself. Prayers that she be a good steward of the leadership her constituents had given her. That was powerful and specific.

And while many of the needs were similar from ward to ward, the idea is for us to pray for the specific ward, regardless of crossover needs. If we need to pray for poverty to be eradicated in 15 different wards, that's what we're going to do.

Preach Where You Reach! I reached city councillors in my position. I used that relationship to articulate my faith, show concern for the issues facing their constituents and offer a supernatural solution. Where do you reach? What relationships have you established that can be used to build God's Kingdom?

For the golf scramble fundraiser that benefits our youth ministry, I truly preached where I reached. Donations from my relationships came in from a bank, web design company, a bus company, television studio, car dealership, banquet center, hotels, public relations firm, real estate company, soft drink company, wine company, equestrian center, record label, an international rock band and more. All fruit from a seed of kindness that was watered by intent and investment.

If you feel like you haven't built any substantial relationships, I encourage you to begin. Invite someone in the business community out to lunch or coffee (or a chai tea latte non-fat, in my case). Don't just ask for favors without building the relationship first. Connect before you expect! Truly get to know peers or clients in a deeper way. Does their daughter take tap lessons? Does their son play baseball? Does their wife love Ryan Gosling? Of course, who's wife doesn't love Ryan Gosling, right? But I digress. When you get to know customers or suppliers in a more authentic way, you can water that relationship with articles, funny memes or video clips specific to that person's hobbies or passions. Maybe even throw in an autographed Ryan Gosling picture for good measure.

When you lead by proactively investing in relationships, you are bringing Jesus to work.

eight

Baseballs in the Cemetery

1 Thessalonians 5:11 (NLT)

"So encourage each other and build each other up, just like you are already doing"

Baseballs in the Cemetery

Between the ages of eight and twelve, I played baseball in a youth program in Loch Raven, Maryland. I absolutely loved playing baseball. I was on the Red Sox which, as a Baltimore Orioles fan, was a shot in the gut but I wore that uniform proudly. I played second base and catcher, mostly, with an occasional stint in the outfield. We played primarily at two ballparks, Oakleigh and Pleasant Plains. Even now, the smell of the glove leather, the crack of the bat and grass-stained white pants can take me right back to my youth. My son, Dublin, played rep/travel baseball for Hamilton's elite baseball team, the Hamilton Cardinals. As a result, I get my fair share of those very youth-reflecting moments. Especially the grass-stained white pants! On a side note, whoever thought white was a good color for outdoor youth sports uniforms?!

Whenever we played on one particular diamond at Pleasant Plains, there was an exciting yet creepy feeling that came over me. For some reason still elusive to me, there was a small, fenced-in cemetery right in the middle of center field. *I'm actually serious.* The mini-cemetery had maybe seven headstones and a large tree. I love how such an obstacle might have been a deterrent for many baseball field planners, but whoever designed this diamond thought, "I can work around it!"

For me and my teammates, the idea of hitting the ball into the cemetery was thrilling. To us, it would seem like a grand-slam. Technically it would be a ground rule double but, in our minds, it was a goal worth pursuing. I hit the ball off the fence a few times but never made it inside the cemetery itself. I probably would have felt bad if I got the ball inside the cemetery. After all they're trying to rest.

Our coaches had a tradition of handing out a game ball to a player at the end of games for a clutch offensive or defensive accomplishments as a means of encouragement. While I was fortunate enough to get a few of these over the years, I seem to only have two in my possession. One ball says "Key catch in center field to prevent run from scoring". The other ball is actually for two separate games. Part of the ball says "Knocked in winning run" in a 13-12 Red Sox victory over the Pirates. The other part of the ball says "Knocked in winning runs" in a 13-12 victory over the Twins. Strange that both victories were 13-12. Perhaps even stranger is that one game ball has two separate games written on it. Truth is, these words could have been written on a napkin and they would have meant just as much to me. While these balls were meant to honor great plays, they were really a tool for speaking encouragement into my life and the lives of my teammates.

I'm sure you've felt discouraged at some point in your childhood and someone came along and spoke words of encouragement into your situation and your life. I know I needed that on occasion in my own childhood. Along came a parent, a teacher, a camp counselor, a friend or a baseball coach and turned my perspective around. But this doesn't stop with our childhood.

Each of us go through days in our personal lives that just beat us up. The workplace is no different. We lose a big account; we miss a formula and the balance sheet is actually worse than we thought; we underwhelm a client with a redesign of the company's logo; we think that big concert is going to happen and then it moves into the next year and now the budget has taken a big hit. That last example was my world and for years it crushed me. Since I invited Christ into my life, I look at those situations and believe that something good and better will come along. Or there is a lesson in that failure for me to learn. But I'm Christ-filled and most people we work with won't share that optimism and hope.

As Christian leaders in the workplace, it is our duty to lift those around us. Saved and unsaved alike. We breathe life into our employees. When things look dark, as Christian leaders, we are the light.

Late one evening, our workplace offices were broken into and vandalized. As the leader in our organization, I knew that I had the responsibility to allay fears and concerns and unify my staff. I also knew that I had to communicate Christ-like optimism during this dark time. I sent an email to my staff that read:

"Good morning! As you may be aware, the offices were vandalized and burglarized on Saturday afternoon. While we incurred some damage and some lost items, I am grateful that no one from our staff was harmed. Whenever something like this occurs, there can be a feeling of being violated, trespassed on. We can get angry, especially if personal items are missing. I just encourage you to not let this weekend discourage you. We are so much greater than those that did this. As a team, we remain resilient and strong. We'll get our

stuff fixed or replaced. Those that did this are clearly broken and desperate.

I have already spoken with the City about the need for cameras inside our office areas. We will be putting other safety measures in place as well. The police will continue to investigate this matter and they will keep us updated in their progress.

We are doing amazing things in this city and this certainly isn't going to slow us down! Keep up the great work!"

The next day, we had our weekly staff meeting. The break-in was the first topic. As I reiterated what I said in the email, one of my employees shared a concern that likely reflected what others were thinking and feeling. She wanted me to understand that, in spite of my optimism and encouragement, she felt uneasy. She felt unsafe. She didn't want those very real feelings to be buried in the avalanche of hope and light. As a Christian leader, it would be easy to dismiss her feelings as coming from someone who needs the peace that I know Jesus brings. But I have to recognize that not everyone has

Jesus as their anchor through these storms. Not everyone is in relationship with Jesus. And in the absence of that relationship and truth, these type of situations can seem scary. I have to understand my audience and let the Holy Spirit guide my words and actions to show them the peace and light of Jesus Christ.

Your employees and co-workers need the same thing. They need you to be the anchor in their storm. But understand, what they really need is the Jesus in you as their anchor. They may not have acknowledged Christ in their lives just yet, but they will encounter Christ through you.

Encouragement can come in many different forms. You can put an encouragement greeting card in an employees mail slot. You can send flowers thanking an employee for a job well done. You can call them out in a staff meeting and give them praise and encouragement for taking such great care of a client or supplier. You can read an email that demonstrates just how their care affected a customers experience.

I've done all of these things because, not only does it encourage the same behavior, but I truly delight in being able to publicly acknowledge excellence and passion. I shared an email with my staff from an event promoter, during my tenure in the entertainment venues. It read:

"Hope all is well. First off I would like to personally compliment you and your team for helping us pull off a great event last month. Very positive experience in all aspects and we already looking forward to next year. In my 20 some odd years of doing events we have never had partners with such dedication, professionalism and ownership in collectively working towards making the event successful."

I got emails like this a lot. And while receiving these emails was a great thing, they wouldn't have an impact unless I used them to thank and encourage my staff.

One of the first things I did when I first came to Hamilton was to have my staff complete something I call an "Employee Interest Form". This form gives me the basics like name and birthday, but then I ask a few other key questions. Favorite type of food? Favorite restaurants? Favorite music artists? Passions and hobbies? Hidden talents? I do this for a few reasons. Knowing my employees on a more personal level allows us to have a closer relationship; it allows me to thank or encourage them with gift cards to their favorite restaurant or tickets to their favorite band or singer rather than generic gift cards or gift cards to a restaurant they may not particularly enjoy.

I ask for their hobbies or talents so that we can look for opportunities to share in those with them. If an employee is a great photographer on the side, you can have some of their photographs enlarged and framed to hang in your reception area. If you have employees that enjoy baking, you can have a bake-off among employees. If they are passionate about and play rugby, you can gather a few co-workers to go cheer them on during their match.

All of these things can be such a big encouragement for your employees. They feel valued, respected and cared about. When you have an employee that gets discouraged, there is nothing like feeling loved and cared about to turn that mindset around.

Baseballs in the Cemetery

When I was in high school, I was a competitive swimmer. In fact, I was a competitive swimmer as long as I can remember. I likely did backstroke in my mother's womb, at least until I had no room left to move. I was a fish, a dolphin, and any other cliched term for someone who spends a lot of time in the water. I swam year round. In the summer, I swam for Rock Spring Swim Club and in the winter I swam for my high school. In high school I had Mr. Jensen as my coach. And like most coaches, he knew how to critique my performance, but he had the wisdom to understand he needed to add encouragement to his commentary. He helped shape me into the best swimmer I could be. I swam mostly back and fly (backstroke and butterfly for those that aren't familiar with swimming vernacular). And while Mr. Jensen was instrumental in my success in the pool, I received one of the most important moments of encouragement after practice on one particular day.

In my freshmen and sophomore year of high school, I was not able to drive to school. That privilege was for the juniors and seniors. So my mother would pick me up at the entrance to my high school. I had walked out to her car the same way many times before, but on this day, I was about to receive a profound word that would not only change me, but stick with me many, *many* years later. When I got in the car, my mother said "when you walk out to the car, lift your head up. You always look at the ground and I can't see your face."

You're likely thinking, "really? That was the profound word that changed you? Lift your head up?" It's true. She likely doesn't remember what provoked that instruction on that particular day, but I felt it to my core. She was basically saying "lift your head high. Be seen, but more importantly, see! Nothing but an untied shoe happens where you're looking, but while you are doing that, life is passing by. Be proud of who you are and announce to the world, with your head held high, that you matter".

I've never told my mother how that simple encouragement changed me, but it did. If I find myself looking down, I can hear her voice, and I lift my head. Still to this day.

Those that we lead are looking for us to put our figurative finger on their chin and lift their heads up. It's easy to encourage someone when they've done a great job. We say "hey that thing you did, great job, keep that up". But when they've made a mistake, they need us even more. I remember one time in particular, my Director of Finance came to me and let me know about a mistake that her finance team made, under her leadership, and she was upset. I'm sure she was nervous to tell me because it had a financial impact on the business. She explained the situation and apologized. I said "ok, so we know what was done wrong and we've put measures in place to prevent it from happening again. So just adjust the financials and we'll move on". She said "I really thought you would rip into me for the mistake". I said "you're a great Director of Finance. This was clearly a mistake, an oversight. We all make them. Yelling at you wouldn't change the situation. We just need to make sure it doesn't happen again". She thanked me for being so understanding and grateful for my compassion.

We've all been there. We've all made mistakes, missed deadlines, screwed up an order, failed to communicate properly and cost our businesses money. But our God is greater than any mistake we could make. And it is our responsibility to have our God show through us even in, perhaps especially in, the face of adversity.

Preach Where You Reach: Bring Your Jesus to Work (*Every*) Day

In approximately AD 50, Paul wrote a letter to the Thessalonians. The relatively new church was concerning themselves with when Christ would return. Paul wanted to encourage them to remain faith-filled and focus on Jesus and His teachings, not his pending return. The timing of the return of Christ would be unexpected, he explained, but as believers, His return itself would not be unexpected. Paul was not only encouraging them, but he wanted them to continue to encourage one another. Paul tells them to be clearheaded, protected by the armor of faith and love and encourage each other and build each other up.

Isn't that the picture of the modern day church as well? Surrounded by faith-filled believers that encourage and build each other up. And as believers, shouldn't we be the Paul in our workplaces? While we don't likely have the freedom to encourage our employees to keep their minds and hearts on Jesus, we can pour out the the same Paul-like encouragement from the Christ within us. Your employees may not know Christ, but they know you. And that should be as close a facsimile as possible. You're not just a leader, you're a Christian leader. There's power and responsibility in that.

Baseballs in the Cemetery

Everyone wants to feel like they matter; like they have done a great job or that their boss believes in them. The saved and unsaved all look for validation. Though the Bible tells us we are fearfully and wonderfully made, even as Christians, we sometimes struggle to believe that. This is especially so if we actually make a mistake. Imagine those in your workplace without Jesus and without the hope He brings. How difficult must it be for them? We all desire to do a good job and contribute to the success of our workplace. And when we fail, we need a leader that can lift us up and speak encouragement into us.

So imagine you have a baseball. A game ball. Who are you giving it to? What are you writing on it? I still have mine, forty years later. Who are you telling to lift their head up? What simple words will you use that will have a decades-long impact? When confronted with an employee's mistake, what words of life are you speaking into them and the situation?

Don't limit your words of encouragement to only your employees. If you are truly going to preach where you reach, you need to be an encourager to everyone your positions places in your path - the elevator repair contractor, the landscaping company worker, the radio account executive, the IT contractor and so on. Everyone experiences discouragement in their jobs. Let the Christ within you, lift the chins of everyone around you.

When you lead with encouragement, you are bringing Jesus to work.

nine

Traveling Blues & Horse-shoes

1 Thessalonians 5:18 (NLT)

"Be thankful in all circumstances, for this is God's will for you who belong to Christ Jesus."

Traveling Blues & Horseshoes

Throughout my entertainment career, I traveled to New York, Los Angeles and Nashville annually. I love to travel. Well, not exactly. I love the idea of traveling. There's something exciting about being in a city away from home with so much to discover. New restaurants, shopping, museums, live music. The list goes on. But getting to that destination, well that's another story.

I'm a "rather be an hour early than a minute late" kinda guy. So I get up early and have my wife, or a car service, take me to the airport. After a kiss goodbye, with my wife not the car service, that would just be awkward, I have to stand in a line to check my bags. Then I'm off to stand in the forever-long security line, zig zagging back and forth like I'm queuing up for some less than exciting ride at Disney World. After making it through security, it's off to wait at the a gate. Finally it's time to board the plane and we make our way, at a turtle-like pace, into the aircraft. I eventually make it to my window seat where I prepare my reading material and my music. I'm ready for take-off, but inevitably there's a delay. Waiting for a passenger to arrive, stocking up the Bloody Mary mix, topping off the fuel or a mechanical issue. I've heard them all. In the cases of the fuel and the mechanical issue, I don't mind them taking as much time as they need, let's be honest.

And then we are off! Once we hit our cruising altitude, I get lost in the music of Hillsong United, Elevation, Jesus Culture or Bethel while I read the latest offering by Judah Smith, Steven Furtick or TD Jakes. And I'm at peace. I get filled with an overwhelming sense of gratitude. When I focus on Jesus, through worship music or a God-inspired word, I begin to appreciate the woman at the check-in counter, the security staff and the gate agent. I look past my frustrations and begin to see just how amazing it is that I have the opportunity and ability to leave one city, fly through the air, and arrive in a city thousands of miles away a few hours later. I look back at the snail-like pace of my morning and I see Jesus. I see Him slowing me down to help me appreciate just how wonderful the experience of traveling actually can be.

In our busy lives, we can be so focused on ourselves and what we are trying to achieve that we have a hard time appreciating what we've already accomplished. We can get so wrapped up in the accomplishment itself that we forget about those that helped us achieve it. We can be so bottom-line focused that we neglect to express our gratitude to those that were so passionate, dedicated and skillful in allowing that success to come to fruition.

Traveling Blues & Horseshoes

About seven years ago, I came to Hamilton with a few Directors intent on impacting a city. The culture had to be created from scratch. We had seeds to plant in the community. Seven years later, the fruit of seeding into relationships and corporate partnerships is evident and abundant. But I could not have done it without my Directors. On our four year anniversary, I sent emails to each of my Directors, thanking them. I sent the following email to my Director of Marketing:

"Good morning and Happy Anniversary! Can you believe it's been 4 years since we came to Hamilton to start this next chapter of our careers? I remember being in Cleveland and calling you and chatting about Hamilton on many occasions. There was excitement but also a bit of the unknown. Especially for me, moving to another country. I didn't know any of my Directors, with the exception of you. And I only knew you a little bit. I have to say that having you join me in Hamilton was the best decision I could have made. I am so incredibly grateful for your leadership, energy, passion and knowledge. You have been instrumental in our success and I just want to say thank you. I am certainly

grateful to have you on my team, but I more grateful to have you in my life. Thank you for your friendship. We have come a long way from the angry town halls in the very beginning! I look forward to many more years together.

I can't accurately articulate what you mean to me, but I will just say – from the bottom of my heart – thank you. Thank you for taking a chance on me, and Hamilton. I know it wasn't easy. I still can't believe you did it, if I'm being honest. But I wouldn't be the same person I am today without you starting the journey with me."

I may have lead the organization, but I could not do it alone. I needed strong leaders on the Director level as well. And those Directors had to believe in and deliver the culture that I wanted, to those whom they lead. Those leaders needed to know and feel that they were respected and valued. But I didn't just say "hey thanks for your hard work". I expressed sincere, authentic gratitude because I felt it in my core.

Let's admit, gratitude is easier when you have an amazing team around you and business is great. When everyone is firing on all cylinders and you're landing new clients and profits are strong, we find a way to squeak out a "thanks everybody". But what about when there are struggles in fiscal performance? What about the times when employees make mistakes? What about when everything seems to be falling down around us? Can we still express gratitude?

1 Thessalonians 5:18 (NLT) says *"Be thankful in all circumstances, for this is God's will for you who belong in Christ Jesus". All circumstances. And it's God's will for you! As believers, we know that good can come from even the most difficult, adverse situations. In Romans 8:28 the Bible tells us "And we know that God causes everything to work together for the good of those who love God and are called according to His purpose for them."* This is a God promise!

That's not to say that we won't feel disappointment when we fall short of budget. That's not to say that we won't feel frustrated when our top performer makes mistakes. That's not to say that we won't feel discouraged when our boss beats us down. But as a Christian leader, we aren't focused on what we feel. We are focused on God's truth. Regardless of circumstances, there is an opportunity to be radically thankful. In every negative situation, not only can we find something to be grateful for, but we know that God will turn the situation around for the good of those who love Him.

My first marriage ended in divorce. It was one of the darkest periods of my life. Not because the marriage was ending, though that was painful, but I knew it meant I wouldn't be with my two daughters on a daily basis. I couldn't bare the thought of being without them, not tucking them in at night, not helping with their home-work. I knew I would miss milestones, activities and bel-ly-laughs. I felt completely hollow. I remember laying on the laundry room floor, curled up in the fetal position and crying until my head pulsated with pain. I wanted to end my life in that moment. Missing these moments because I was no longer living was better than missing them alive, I thought. While this struggle was before I accepted Christ into my life, I have no doubt that He was in the midst of my pain, carrying me through it.

The pain was real. I missed concert band performances, softball games, parent/teacher conferences and so much more. And yet I remain incredibly grateful. My ex-wife

Traveling Blues & Horseshoes

remarried and she and her husband raised my daughters and they deserve a lot of credit for shaping them into the extraordinary women they are today. My oldest daughter, Kaileigh, was an outstanding member of the University of Delaware Marching Band. I never thought I'd love the clarinet so much! My daughter, Karleigh, has had significant athletic achievement in both softball and field hockey. But beyond their God-given gifts, they are compassionate, smart and funny. They fill my life with so much joy.

I also remarried. My wife, Whitney, and I have two children of our own. Berkleigh, our daughter, has an enormous passion for horses and, as a result, I've had to learn to spell equestrian. Horse rider is easier but doesn't sound nearly as sophisticated. Berkleigh also has a tremendous singing voice and has begun singing worship at our church. She's also a gifted piano player and artist. God was really stacking her gifting pile high. He's got big plans for this girl! Our son, Dublin, is a phenomenal athlete, regardless of sport, and often reminds me about the time we played golf when he was nine. He parred the par 3. I shot four on the hole. But I shot better than him on the next hole and rubbed it in his little nine-year-old face. Sad, I know.

God is amazing! He took a broken marriage, an aborted suicide and emotional pain and turned it into four extraordinary children that are growing in their relationship with the Lord. He took a broken-hearted dad, made that heart whole and filled it with gratitude.

My story isn't unique. The people you lead in your workplace may very well have a similar story of pain and sadness. We've all gone through setbacks and paths that led us into darkness. But as a Christian leader, you have the opportunity, I would even say the mandate, to be the light for them. You have the chance to let them know that what they've been through only prepared them for the great things to come. You can assist in shifting their thinking from suffering to gratitude.

You don't need to be at rock bottom to get a revelation of gratitude. Always look for opportunities to tell your employees how thankful you are for what they do for the organization. I certainly think leading with gratitude during adversity can be powerful, but don't neglect the same leadership when things have gone well.

Our arena hosted an NHL exhibition game and an OHL (Ontario Hockey League) game back to back. Both games had specific needs in terms of in-ice logos and other game day requirements. Our crew had to work hard to convert from one event to the next. And they were fantastic. I sent the following email to my staff:

"I wanted to take a moment to say THANK YOU for all the effort leading up to the NHL game, during the game and the changeover from NHL to OHL. When a promoter says 'Can we do that?', whatever the request is, my immediate reaction is 'Absolutely'. It's not because I know, it's because I know you! Time and time again you rise to the challenge.

Whether it's our conversion crew, our ice building (and shaving) guys, our cleaning crew, our box office staff, our "all hands on deck" full-time staff, dedicated part-time staff, maintenance/electrical...the list goes on – we get the job done, and well. Now, you could say, "that's our job" and yes, you'd be right. But you deserve thanks and praise for getting it done so quickly and with such heart and passion. We don't go through the motions here. We put in an effort that is multiplied because we take pride in our work. It's a reflection of who we are as individuals and as a team. So, thank you. I continue to be grateful for all that you do!"

We did so many events over the course of a year that my staff could do this work in their sleep. It would be easy to take it for granted and move on to the next event. But I wouldn't have a Christ-centered culture if I allowed that to happen. Yes, this work was part of their job. They would do it whether I say thank you or not. But how much sweeter does the accomplishment feel when you are receiving authentic, heartfelt gratitude?

As I mentioned previously, we had Garth Brooks perform five shows in four days. We saw over 80,000 fans come to the shows. It was an enormous undertaking, resulting in a huge economic impact to our city. In a moment of reflection, I, once again, penned an email to express my gratitude. The email read:

"I wanted to take a moment to express my sincere thanks for all the hard work that went into the five Garth shows in four days. These opportunities don't come along often, as you know. It's important that when they do come along, we have attention to detail, pride in our work and a passion for the job. All of you were extraordinary in your roles. When I asked the promoter if he had any feedback on our venue or staff he said simply, "It was all perfect in every way". I am incredibly proud to work alongside each of you. I don't think there's anything that you would let get in the way of creating the best guest/show experience possible. Absolute warriors. Thank you for your detailed planning. Thank you for thinking on your feet and being spontaneous. Thank you for the energy you bring to the various teams you oversee. Thank you for not only being so good at your jobs, but for being an inspiration to me still after 26 years in this crazy business".

Your employees want to feel valued and respected. We all do! So how do we best position ourselves to be great leaders that express thanksgiving to our employees? How can we become great givers of gratitude? Well, it all starts with the revelation that God put us in our positions of authority. We have been placed in leadership exactly where we are so that His will can be carried out through us. We may have received a great education and worked extremely hard to get where we are, but understand that God has placed you where you are for His purpose and His glory.

When Paul wrote to the church in Corinth, he made this point very clear. In 1 Corinthians 15:10 (ESV), Paul wrote *"But by the grace of God I am what I am, and his grace toward me was not in vain. On the contrary, I worked harder than any of them, though it was not I, but the grace of God that is with me."*

If you were to come into my church on any given Sunday, you would walk into worship and think a bank robbery was happening. Hands are lifted high, across the entire sanctuary, in surrender, reverence and gratitude. The enormity of what Christ did for us is hard to wrap our heads around. And when the presence of God fills the atmosphere, there's a tangible feeling of overwhelming appreciation for the sacrifice of Jesus.

One song in particular will absolutely destroy me emotionally. When our worship band starts the first few notes of "For The Cross", by Bethel Music, written by Brian Johnson, Gabriel Wilson and Ian McIntosh, I can feel the tears welling up in my eyes. It's not long before the tears stream down my face and I'm practically on my knees, broken from the weight of gratitude for all that Jesus went through for me. I truly believe the more you understand the sacrifice of Jesus, the more grateful you will become. The more grateful you become, the easier it will be to find opportunities to express that gratitude in the workplace. Look for ways to acknowledge the hard work and dedication of your employees. Seek opportunities to express appreciation for your clients, vendors, suppliers, media relationships or tenants. There will always be a chance to articulate thankfulness, in victories and defeats. Don't take these moments for granted. Expressions of gratitude can truly transform a workplace.

When you lead with gratitude, you are bringing Jesus to work.

CONCLUSION

When you bring Jesus to work every day, you can build amazing, fruitful businesses filled with employees that are happy, respected, engaged and productive. You can have suppliers and clients that feel valued and cared about. You can have customers that have trust in your product and your word. And when storms come, and they will, you will have built something that is firmly anchored on the Word and promises of God.

The Christ-like attributes I touched on in this book are simply examples of some of the qualities I've implemented in my workplaces. I could easily add patience, self-control, forgiveness, fairness, courage, honesty and so many more. I encourage you to pick eight to ten Christ-like qualities to start and put them into practice in your respective role. Don't just practice these attributes within your department or within your office building. Let your Christ-centered culture radiate from you in every interaction. I encourage you to Preach Where You Reach! Bring Jesus to work every day.

Conclusion

You don't need to speak about Jesus all the time, but Jesus should be speaking through you daily.

1 John 2:6 (ESV)

"whoever says he abides in him ought to walk in the same way in which he walked"

ACKNOWLEDGEMENTS

This book would not have been possible without the unconditional love and support of so many.

To Whitney: Having you as my wife is an extraordinary blessing I could never deserve, but having you as my best friend leaves me speechless. Your unending encouragement and support during the writing of this book inspired me to keep pushing. You reminded me that God doesn't call the qualified, He qualifies the called. I will be forever inspired by your steadfast and unwavering faith in God.

To my children, Kaileigh, Karleigh, Berkleigh & Dublin: God has extraordinary plans and purposes for your lives. It is my prayer that you step into His purpose for your lives and glorify Him as you thrive and flourish. Wherever God calls you, always keep Christ at the center. I love you so incredibly much.

Acknowledgements

To Pastors Peter & Peggy Rigo: It is impossible to articulate what you have both meant in my life. The presence of God was so palpable at Poema Church that I just raised my hands in surrender and Christ met me there. I gave my life to Christ in this church and my family has been changed forever. Thank you for your continued leadership, support and friendship. I am grateful beyond measure.

To my mother, Virginia (Boots): I first saw Christ through you. You showed me what it was to be unselfish, compassionate, kind, loving, encouraging and have a desire to serve others. Before giving my life to Jesus, I was a disciple of you. Thank you for your example. Thank you for your unconditional love and encouragement. God knew that you were exactly who I needed in my life to shape me and raise me so that one day I would be stepping into my purpose with a solid foundation. I love you like you've loved me, without limitation.

To my father, David Warren: Thank you for helping to shape me into the person I am today. Thank you for singing "Happy Birthday" to me every year without fail. I am so grateful for you and I pray that this book, and my life, lead you into an even deeper relationship with Jesus. He loves you immensely, and I do too.

To all my bosses, co-workers and employees over the years: Each of you has had a profound impact on my life and I am immensely grateful. I pray that you come into your own revelation of God's purpose for your life and live to lift up the name of Jesus.

www.ingramcontent.com/pod-product-compliance
Lightning Source LLC
Chambersburg PA
CBHW051707170526
45167CB00002B/566